Amazon
The Gy

'A delightful book with characters so well written that you feel you have known them for years.'

'-an absorbing story with characters you really care about.'

'The perfect novel to read in the garden on a lazy sunny afternoon with a glass or two of wine.'

'Looking forward to reading more books in the future from this author.'

'Told with such artistic fluency, I felt I was living the story amongst them all.'

'Interesting characters, an engaging plot and an entrancing location.'

Susanna Scott lives in a seaside town on the Yorkshire Coast. She loves her family, gardening, reading and writing books that people might possibly want to read! She has a children's book in the pipeline. The Winterfell Stone is her second novel.

Also by Susanna Scott
The Gypsy Caravan

Susanna Scott @yorkshirecoastwriter
on Facebook

Chapter 1

'Meadow Cottage? It's only down the road. I reckon you could walk it, no problem. Case is on wheels isn't it?'

The grey-haired, grizzled-looking taxi driver was looking through his horn-rimmed spectacles at Annie's case and seeing a small, doll-size valise whereas she saw a large sea chest-size object.

'It's really heavy' she tried with a sigh that invited sympathy but earned a shake of the head instead. How many taxi drivers turned custom away? Had she arrived on another planet? She took a sneaky sniff under one arm in case that was the problem.

'Big strong girl like you, it'd be no problem.'

'What are you trying to say here?' Annie looked down at her average height, average build figure in alarm but just caught the twinkle in the driver's eye. She leaned towards him.

'Look, between ourselves, there's a heavy case full of gold bullion at my feet and if you'll be my getaway driver, I'll give you a generous tip.'

He chuckled as he pulled the case towards the boot of his taxi while Annie grinned. Were they all like this in Winterfell? She hoped so.

After strapping herself in the passenger seat, she listened to his running commentary as he drove at ten miles per hour. Annie looked behind but there were no other cars on the road to be held up by his snail's pace. He pointed out landmarks such as –

'There's the bakers with the tea shop next door. That's what your new neighbours ran before they retired. Best Victoria Sponge in the Dales. That there's a newsagent cum ironmongers and you'll find everything there, including the kitchen sink. There's the hairdressers…'

He stopped talking and gave her a sidelong glance taking in her shoulder-length dirty blonde curls that did their own thing in any direction they chose.

'Don't reckon they'll know what to do with you though.' he winked.

Annie gasped theatrically but then burst out laughing, spoiling the 'affronted' effect.

Literally two minute later, after taking a left past the Hunter's Moon pub on the corner and up the narrow Bank Lane climbing out of the village, the taxi stopped outside Meadow Cottage.

'You went slowly to make it seem further, didn't you?' she laughed.

'Got to give you your money's-worth, guided tour included.' he smiled, dragging the case onto the pavement while Annie manhandled the rucksack, looking for her purse.

'How much…?'

'Nothing' he said putting his hand up, 'call it a welcome to Winterfell. I told you that you'd could have easily walked it.'

Annie couldn't believe it, she felt at home already although he might just be the best of a really bad bunch of clique-y villagers. She turned to look at the lane they'd just driven up.

'I'd never have pulled the case up the hill, it's pretty steep.'

'You could have stopped at the bank and deposited your gold bullion first? You can buy me a half in the pub if you ever go in.'

'I most certainly will...' she hesitated, feeling like she should know his name already.

'Frank' he responded, holding his hand out.

'I'm Annie.' She shook his hand enthusiastically.

'Annie Millford, aye, I know. Tom and Ada told me.' He nodded towards a neighbouring house. 'You'll like them. Lovely couple.'

Annie was sure she would but also quite sure that she wouldn't be able to make a move without being watched and becoming an entry in a secret notebook. *"A' went down lane today. 10am. Wearing a black jacket and a shifty expression'*

'Well, it's a revelation' she said 'A taxi driver trying to turn away trade and then not charging. I'm very grateful.'

He pulled the car door open, plonked himself inside and leaned towards her.

'Oh, I'm not the taxi driver love' he indicated the sign on the roof 'I just borrowed it from Aidan next door to me so I could get the wife to her train on time. That's why you saw me outside the station. I'm a plumber.'

His shoulders shook in silent mirth as he saw the expression on her face, then he turned the taxi round up the hill and waved casually on the way back down. Annie could just about manage to wave back, caught between embarrassment and wanting to double up with laughter.

She turned towards the terraced cottage, her new home for the next year.

Meadow Cottage was the middle cottage of three in a terrace called Bank Farm Terrace, all built in a mellowed limestone which made it look sunny even on a late November day like today. The house on the left, Field View, was fully attached to hers and the one on the right, Hillside, was separated by a passageway which belonged to her, for ease of access to her back garden and door without going over anyone else's land. In the space above this passage, there was an extra bedroom, which she had earmarked for her study, although she had only seen the photos in the brochure so far. This bedroom, as well as the whole terrace, overlooked the church which was directly across the road from it but set back in the grounds.

All three cottages had wrought-iron railings set in a low stone wall, enclosing small front gardens which Annie imagined would be full of flowers in Spring but now just looked sad and bare. She caught sight of a yellow rose or two clinging to the walls, their leaves climbing over the little half-porch. This was open at the sides apart from trellis panels but was just enough for you to shelter from the rain while you found your key.

More than anything, it was Annie's escape for a year. A retreat to collect her thoughts and decide what she wanted to do now. A sanctuary, she hoped, from the life she had left behind.

Heaving a sigh that seemed to come up from her boots, she knocked at the door of Hillside - her neighbours Tom and Ada's house - whose names she now knew courtesy of the taxi-driving plumber, to collect her key.

Chapter 2

Annie made her coffee the next morning with the last UHT sachet from her welcome pack. She needed to go to the shops but didn't want to miss the removal men. When she said removal men, she meant Pete and Alan, builders extraordinaire, who had borrowed a white van from somewhere and had offered to do the job as they could visit their mum in Skipton at the same time. She had gone to school with them around fifteen years ago now and had lived just down the road from them for the last ten. Her best friend Lettie lived nearby too until she married and moved to Scotland.

There wasn't much to bring from her house in Cambersea as she was letting it out furnished and this cottage was furnished too. It was stuff such as clothes, including warm winter coats, her laptop and her workstation, which was going under the window in the study. There were books, personal items, art equipment, books, wellies, books, her favourite mug and casserole dish and more books. Her Kindle was pressed to use on the train yesterday but she still preferred the feel of paper as she turned the page and the pleasure of choosing a new book from a bookshop instead of it getting delivered electronically. Besides, a Kindle would never smell the same as a new book.

Meadow Cottage had been used as a holiday house by the owners, purely for their own use but they had gone to Australia for a year to visit family so this arrangement was perfect for both of them.

She looked around her at the kitchen-diner. It was a large room for such a small cottage but didn't have much in the way of work surfaces unless you counted the table, which the owners obviously did. Annie didn't profess to be a cordon bleu cook so it would do her nicely. She could see it becoming her favourite place. The sun's rays were already sneaking their way onto the large pine table placed near the back wall with a wooden settle behind it. The table had collapsible leaves at each end and a long cushioned wooden bench, shoved under the side away from the settle. There was a large carver chair with a crocheted throw at each side of the fireplace. Considering it would mostly just be her eating here, it was definitely seating overload. She felt she should invite some people round just so the seating got used.

The butler's sink was set under a long low window. When she was washing up, she would be able to see down the long garden and onto the fields and the fells beyond them. There was a large panelled glass door next to it leading out onto a little patio area. She hadn't explored the outdoor area yet.

The piece de resistance though was the black kitchen stove in the fireplace. It wasn't an Aga as it had a brass plaque above with The Yorkshire Range Company engraved on it. There was an overmantel incorporated with a drying rail and two engraved pillars at the sides. At the left was a hotplate with a large kettle on it, presumable you could keep the water hot indefinitely with just topping it up? At the right was a large oven with brass fittings and a separate griddle coming out at the front. The best part was the open fire in the middle, with a spit fitted on hooks above it. Annie felt that there should be a cauldron hanging from it.

She had gone through the house earlier, choosing how she would use the rooms. The snug sitting room at the front caught the sun early in the morning so it would be a nice place for her breakfast spot on the small table under the window with its two wheelback chairs, overlooking the church. There were two comfortable armchairs, one set to the left of the woodburning stove, set in an old limestone fireplace. Against the back wall was a cherry red sofa which had seen better days and was now disguised by a cream throw. It was so nice and squashy to flop out on though. A small TV was set in the recess to the right of the fire a matching comfortable chair was set back redundantly against the adjoining kitchen wall as though no one could possibly have more than three visitors at once. The door out of this room led into a tiny lobby with the stairs leading up from it and a selection of coat hooks on the wall, ranging from a tasteful wooden rack with wrought iron hooks to two Mickey and Minnie mouse hooks, which might have been for their children before one of them grew up and decided to emigrate to Australia. There was also a hook made up of a dog's tail with a mournful looking dog's head looking backwards at it. Unless the dog wore a raincoat- and some did – she imagined it was to hang a lead on.

She went over to the fire in the stove to see how to light it. She was a beginner at all this as she was used to just turning a dial for the heating to come on. There was central heating here but it was apparently fed by the stove. She would follow the instructions later. For now, she pulled her thick cardigan around her and wrote 'fire lighters' on her shopping list along with 'food'.

Thinking of this, she remembered the lovely stew she had eaten last night which warmed her through as she sat in front of the portable convector heater she found and thanked her lucky stars for. The stew had been brought round ten minutes after she had arrived. A little woman who incredibly turned out to be in her eighties, said she needn't cook on her first night now. She had alert, twinkly eyes and was tiny in height and build with silver hair in a wispy bun. She introduced herself as Maisie, her neighbour from Field View. When thanked profusely by Annie who had only got a prepacked sandwich to eat for her dinner, she said she was very welcome and she hoped she would enjoy her time here, then she scuttled back home with Annie's fervent thanks ringing in her ears.

Annie had previously collected, along with the key, one of the famous Victoria sponge cakes, which deserved Frank's accolades. Tom and Ada had welcomed her warmly too and said they were here if she needed them but they wouldn't be round every five minutes 'mithering' her so she didn't need to worry. Annie wondered if she'd given them the impression that she was unapproachable but it turned out that the owners of her cottage had told them that Annie was here to work at home. Which was true, she supposed, as soon as she got her head round it.

Tom was tall but spare, full of smiles and kindness whereas Ada, with her grey permed hair and flowered pinny was slightly more no-nonsense and practical. It was nice to know that both neighbours were so lovely. They hadn't asked for her life story either, though that might come later.

There was a knock at the door and Annie swallowed the rest of her coffee before she went to greet Pete, Alan - and her books.

Chapter 3

It was nearly midday by the time the brothers had unloaded the van, had a cup of tea, put the world to rights and roared off to see their mum.

Annie had made a cursory attempt at putting things in the right place but a loud rumble she at first thought was coming from the pipes, proved to be her empty stomach loudly telling her it hadn't had any breakfast.

She ran down the stairs and grabbed her parka from the hook and closed the door to the sitting room on her left, ostensibly to keep some heat in, although she hadn't actually lit the woodburner yet. She went out into the cold air outside, hunching her shoulders in protest. She put the key in the outside of the door, looking up the lane to her right as she did. There was a figure walking down the lane which was strange as there were no more houses past Ada and Tom's only the sweeping hills and dales as far as the eye could see. Perhaps he was just out for a walk, although he definitely didn't seem to be wearing standard walking gear. As he came nearer, she saw what appeared to be a tramp – a homeless man who wanted to be homeless with the freedom to wander. There had been one who came to Cambersea a couple of times a year- very intelligent and well-educated – but had chosen that life after a trauma that he had only hinted at and never explained.

This man was a little closer now and she could see his long, army-style coat which had seen better days, skimming his ankles, with the collar turned up past his ears. He had an old knitted scarf wound a couple of times round his neck and wore a strange brimmed hat. She couldn't tell if it was made of leather or just shiny with age.

She turned back so as not to stare and pulled the door shut with a slam which sent the key flying out and into the rose bushes on the right. Typical, thought Annie, thorns tearing my parka before she realised it wouldn't make any difference anyway as it was so old and the fur on the hood was wearing away. The key wasn't hooked on the branches that she could see so she knelt down and scrabbled around in the rose leaf - covered soil until she felt the metal under her fingers. She stood up triumphantly, locked the door and turned to see the tramp just passing her gate

He was looking curiously at her, which was a cheek, she thought, as he looked like a disturbing cross between Dr Who, Sherlock Holmes -and Worzel Gummidge. If she was being kind, there was a slight Poldark effect too, which probably came from the brown eyes and dark winged eyebrows which were all she could see of his face. She was shocked to see that he didn't look much older than her with his dark brown curls flopping over his forehead.

'Good morning' she stammered, wrong-footed, then checked her watch, 'yes, still morning, just.'

The Tramp's face broke into a smile, at least his eyes crinkled. He took his hat off and bowed down like a courtier, sweeping the hat close to the ground.

'And a good morning to you too, dear lady.' he replied in a deep, mellifluous voice – and replacing the hat, he continued down the lane.

Annie smiled after him, she couldn't help it as he had such a cheerful air about him. She knew there would be a story there, a reason why he would prefer a life on the road to whatever he had before. as there had been with Old Ken at Cambersea. It was probably traumatic too but it seemed he'd managed to keep cheerful, which was a blessing.

As she pulled her hood up against the cold, she dislodged some yellow rose petals that must have been caught in her hair during the key hunt. No wonder he was staring at her, she must have looked like Carmen Miranda or a faded Hippie Flower Child. She put her other arm through the empty rucksack and went into the Winterfell village high street for provisions.

*

Annie soon discovered that the village had everything she needed despite the shops all being on one long main street. Strangely – and pleasingly – there wasn't even a supermarket unless you counted the one attached to the garage beyond the railway station. You could get all you needed from the butchers, which doubled as a pie shop and the baker's which doubled as a tea shop. In the absence of a candlestick maker, you could buy candlesticks, along with the candles to go in them, from Clegg's ironmongers cum newsagent. There was a greengrocer which sold local produce and a marvellous deli, well-stocked with a huge variety of cheeses and cold meats and lots of local honey, jam and pickles too. It also sold alcohol although, checking the prices only after she'd put the wine in her basket, Annie thought she might be better making a few trips to the garage shop for that. Swinging the now full rucksack, which included a very enticing chicken and ham pie for her lunch, onto her back, she made her way home.

As she approached the Hunter's Moon Inn on the corner of Bank Lane, she noticed the tramp sitting on one of the tables outside. There was nothing in front of him on the table and he sat with his eyes closed as if tired and in pain. On a whim, Annie went through the pub door. There were quite a few people in and an enticing smell came from the kitchens. There were alcoves lit by faux gas lamps and a roaring fire blazed away on the far wall, which unsurprisingly was where most of the customers were gathered. She didn't notice Frank the plumber amongst them. The rosy-cheeked landlord stopped wiping a glass.

'What can I get you?' he smiled.

'It's not for me but there's a man with a brimmed hat on sitting at one of your outside tables. I wonder, before he takes off, can I buy a bowl of soup and a pot of tea for him? I'll pay for it now but don't tell him it was me. Also, do you know Frank the plumber?'

The landlord nodded slowly, seemingly entranced by the strange turn his day was taking.

'Well can I pay for a pint for him too please? You can tell him it's from Annie Millford.'

He wrote the orders down on separate pieces of paper then raised his eyes to her, pen in hand.

'Anyone else you want to buy for before I take this through?' he asked with a twinkle in his eye.

Annie wasn't quite sure if he meant it.

'Unless you'd like a pint as well?' she offered, seriously.

He burst out laughing.

'No, I was only kidding you love. I'm Trevor – and you're the new tenant of Meadow Cottage?'

Annie grinned back at him.

'Yes, has the pigeon post called by then?'

'No, we yodel news from the hills round here. We find it's quicker and doesn't make a mess on the pavements.'

'That's me out then' laughed Annie 'I had to drop out of my yodelling course.'

They were both still grinning as Annie paid for everything and went through the door with a cheeky wave for Trevor.

She saw the man was still sitting there thank goodness, lost in thought. He came to as she passed and recognising her, tipped his hat in greeting again, the eyes smiling above the scarf.

'Hello again' she said before turning the corner.

As soon as she began walking up the lane, she started worrying. Some of these people were very

26

proud and refused offers of help. Would he be offended at what she perceived as a kindness and what he might see as an insult? Oh well, too late, it was done now. She was also slightly shaken, seeing his dark curls again, at how much a tramp could look disconcertingly like Ross Poldark!

Half way up the hill, she crossed the road to examine the old red brick building next to the church gardens. She called them gardens as she couldn't see any graves here but had noticed some from her upstairs office, all to the left and the back of the church itself. This brick building was probably Victorian and had a sign saying 'Library', and another sign with the same word on an arrow pointing to the left. Above the door, carved into the stone lintel were the words The Winterfell Institute. Around the corner, the building was separated from the church land by a narrow through lane, which was thankfully one-way. Walking further along the lane, she could see the library had a modern extension at the back, mostly glass, and the big sliding door was now the entrance. She would come back here another time, just to have a look at what they offered. Meanwhile, a chicken and ham pie was beckoning.

Lithvhen Castle
NW Highlands
Scotland

My Dearest Grandson
It was so lovely to see you last week. You are so very welcome anytime you are up this way, something I can't say to most people as they very rarely get this far North!

You are looking well and it was very nice of you to say that we hadn't changed, although I'm sure we have. Old age catches up with us all.

I did notice though that you had that furrow between your eyebrows again, so you are worrying about something? Let me know if we can help as we want you to be the carefree boy of old. I know realistically this cannot be as we all have to grow up and your career is a very interesting, if demanding one. We hope it hasn't made your life too busy, travelling all over the country?

Your grandfather is looking over my shoulder and saying I worry too much! You know what I'm like. He also says to bring a good bottle of Glenmorangie up next time as you drunk all his! (And we know he drank most of it himself!)

We both love you very much and look forward to more visits now you have business up here.
G and G xxx

Chapter 4

It was another bitterly cold day but luckily, Annie had got the hang of the Yorkshire Range by now and it was on a low heat permanently, day and night. It was in front of this source of warmth that she now sat huddled over eating a slice of toast. Her ideas about breakfast at the table in the sitting room sunshine had gone by the board as there was no sunshine and it didn't seem as inviting. She had decided to only light the wood burner when she went in to watch TV as it was a shame to waste the kitchen's warmth. The spotlight above the range was switched on, lending an extra bit of comfort to this dark morning.

She didn't feel much like going out into the grey day and she really ought to start arranging her things in the study room upstairs but she had promised herself a trip to the library and it was only down the lane. She was conscious that, although she was looking for things going on in the village as well as for books, she didn't really want to get too involved as that was what had overwhelmed her in her home town.

Wiping the crumbs from her mouth, she grabbed her trusty parka from the lobby, first checking for any stray rose petals in the hood and ventured outside before she changed her mind.

The wind blew icy arrows of rain in her face as she crossed over to the library and down to the side entrance. She jiggled from one foot to the other whilst waiting for the sliding doors to open, which they did in a maddeningly slow and stately manner. She jumped into a warm open atrium area and to her left was a modern room with the large glass windows making it very light. There were aesthetically displeasing, blue plastic chairs in rows and a sign on the door saying Meeting Room.

To her right was a larger room with a staircase next to it. The room was much darker and obviously part of the original Victorian building which fronted the lane. She could make out desks with computers on them. One was lit up, with an elderly woman seated there, staring intently at the screen.

Ahead of her now was the library proper, which was a much larger room than the others. It was a modern extension again with what looked like glass and chrome bookshelves.

Annie moved forward to the double door and pushed. It didn't move. She pulled but it still didn't move. She looked up to see the librarian. She was a plump lady with a severely short haircut which made her greying hair stand up in places. She was looking at Annie with a totally impassive expression.

She tried the other door but that wouldn't budge either. She searched for a closed sign and not finding one, raised her eyes towards the librarian again, who without changing her expression, made a strange twisting movement with her hand.

Annie was confused and a little outraged – was that some sort of rude sign language she didn't know which was native to the Dales? She glanced down again and saw that the handle, although masquerading as a static one, might actually move. She experimentally gripped the handle and used the twisted hand movement while leaning her weight against the door. It flew open, taking her with it and catapulting her into a bespectacled gentleman who grabbed in vain at the pile of books tumbling out of his hands. She deftly caught two, one in each hand and with a strangled apology, bent down to retrieve the others, registering first the librarian's eyes which were raised heavenward.

Watching the man's rapidly retreating back, she wandered nonchalantly over to the counter.

'I'd like to join the library' she whispered hopefully.

The librarian reached across for a form.

'Do you want to read the books or juggle with them?' she asked, not changing her expression one iota.

Annie hadn't expected humour and produced an explosive bark of laughter. Then, as the woman just continued to stare as she handed the form over, she turned it into a cough, realising it might not have been a joke but a telling off.

'Fill that in' said the woman whose name badge proclaimed her to be 'Minerva'. Of course. It would be. Annie picked up the pen and started to fill the form in.

'I'm only here for a year' she told the Goddess of Wisdom in front of her. The apologetic tone she used was quickly becoming the norm. 'Is that okay?'

There was a short pause and then a nod. After a few seconds, she asked

'Have you just moved into Meadow Cottage?'

'Yes I have.' She smiled encouraged by the slight thaw but the conversation stopped again. Annie tried to keep it moving.

'Very modern isn't it?' She gestured at the minimalistic shelves, 'Not as many books as there used to be either. Quite sparse. Although I suppose a lot of the lending is through e-books online now?

Minerva had stopped what she was doing and was giving Annie one of her special looks, a cross between condescension and pity. Annie rattled on like a runaway train.

'I used to love the libraries when I was little with the shelves overflowing and the smell of polished wood. You could spend hours in there. Much better than...'

She stopped and swallowed hoping that sheer terror would stop her lips from moving or the ice from Minerva's stare would freeze them shut.

'Form's done!' she said with a false brightness and turned to go. She caught sight of a long woollen coat and a striped scarf disappearing into the Meeting Room.

'Oh good, the homeless man has come in to get warm. I wondered how he'd manage in this weather.' said Annie, her smile dying on her lips as Minerva planted her hands firmly on the counter and squeezed her eyes tightly shut. When she opened them, she said in an obviously controlled voice,

'If you mean *Professor* Courtenay, prehistory and archaeology expert at York University, he, while getting warm, is here to prepare for the talk he's giving tonight.'

DIARY

A very odd day today but at least it was more interesting than my usual days in the library.

The new girl from Meadow Cottage came in not long after I'd opened. I say girl, she must be thirty if she's a day but acts a couple of decades younger. She certainly made an impression both on me and poor Mr Cartwright who she nearly knocked over as she opened the door.

She seems pleasant enough, although extremely scatty and accident-prone. A bit of a flibbertigibbet I'd say. Not many brains and probably a lax attitude to life. According to Marje, she's taking a year off. How many people take a year off to do just what they want? Some of us have to work for a living. I wonder if she'll manage not to sustain life-threatening injuries through her clumsiness before she goes back?

She also seems to open her mouth and jam her foot straight in it. She called poor Kit Courtenay a 'homeless man'! The man has letters after his name for heaven's sake. I have to say I can see her point in a way, he is slightly eccentric, both in dress and manner but such a nice man - and so intelligent.

His talk tonight was fascinating. The usual subject of course with the usual suspects attending. The Stone is ancient, part of the village heritage and we need to know more about it, if we weren't stopped at every attempt. Kit had some interesting theories of what it was originally for - as he should of course, for family as well as archaeological reasons.

Of course, with my background, I have more interest in this than most but I don't want that fact to become common knowledge.

Mr Brindleton the vet was there too and he said hello and smiled at me.

One thing about that Annie Millford. She started pulling the library to bits, she preferred the old days. Yes, it does look plasticky but the glass lets in more light and makes it more open. She was right about there being less books - and right about the reason. It does seem a shame. As for the old polished wood she prefers, I can't help but agree with her there. Perhaps she has an old soul, harking back to the past. Who knows?

At least she likes books, which is in her favour of course. I wonder why she is really here?

Chapter 5

This set-up is perfect, thought Annie, although it had taken her nearly all day to sort it out.

The study was set up in the spare bedroom over the passage. The window was a little larger than the other front windows and with her workstation to the left, the morning light fell onto her drawing board as she preferred working in natural light. This left underneath the window free for her to enjoy the window seat on which she now sat, knees drawn up, looking out at the church.

She had experienced a discomfiting encounter on the way back from the library. As if being mortally embarrassed by the scary librarian's revelation about her 'homeless man' wasn't enough. She subsequently tried to avoid him and as she sneaked out onto the lane, the vicar was coming out of the church lych gate, directly opposite her door. He turned and looked her up and down.

'Good morning' she had called, although it really wasn't.

'Will we see you in church?' he replied, not returning her greeting.

Oh no, she thought and stuttered that she was afraid that she didn't actually go to church. Sorry. His face had turned thunderous and turning on his heel he had marched down towards the village, probably to call hell and damnation down on their heads. She could almost feel the horns sprouting out of her own head and resisted moving her hand to her backside to see if she had sprouted a forked tail.

Turning back now, she surveyed her pens, paints and paper with satisfaction. She did all her illustrations on paper first before transferring them digitally onto the screen. She couldn't wait to get started on the new commission. Lettie's children's books were proving to be popular and this year would give her the perfect opportunity to try and make a living at it. Her work on the 'Millie and Maud' books about a pair of rescue sheepdogs had already got her noticed and her agent had received some enquiries about other illustration work.

Annie sighed and set off along the landing wondering if it was respectably late enough for a glass of something alcoholic. She felt exhausted, the past couple of weeks were catching up with her. It should be easier from now on though. She hoped so or there didn't seem much point in making this move. She glanced into the bedroom at the back with its white and gold metal bedframe and the pastel patchwork bedspread. Although slightly smaller than the front bedroom, she chose it because of the wonderful views she would wake up to when she drew the curtains every morning.

Past the end of the three gardens of the terrace, there was the village down to her left and behind the cottages, nothing but uninterrupted views of the countryside. Grazing pastures were directly behind, opening onto a sweeping panorama. A wide valley plain, green and criss-crossed with dry stone walls and then behind that the moorland fells, becoming hazier as they receded into the distance. To her right, just out of her view unless she put her head against the glass, were the hills rising up and along a long brow before they dropped down into the next dale. She could have had this as her study as it was such a light room but she knew she would never get any work done as she would be gazing out of the windows all the time.

In the kitchen Annie opened a bottle of wine, pouring herself a large glass, then she put a ready meal in the oven to cook. She felt she was justified in having a ready meal as it was from the deli, had a posh name and didn't require any preparation. After today, that was a definite requirement. While she waited, hugging the range in one of the carver chairs with its plump, comfy embroidered cushions, she thought about Cambersea, her home town.

She loved the busy seaside town where she had been brought up, with its surge of visitors in summer but lovely wide deserted beaches in winter. She had made it into a cage for herself though and it had reached the point where she wanted to escape to someplace where the activity didn't overload her brain and the traffic didn't mean it meant half an hour to get home.

Cambersea Secondary School was where she had worked as an art teacher more or less straight from art college just over ten years ago. It was a good school and most of the pupils, discounting their short-lived rebellions, were good kids. The odd few had made life a little unpleasant but it wasn't even that - it was all the petty little rules and red tape which had been introduced slowly throughout her time there. Now it had reached saturation point.

Every day there seemed to some new edict that was pointless in the extreme and seemed to be made to justify the existence of the people in their common sense-proof towers, who were solely employed to make life harder than it should be. All this, of course, came at the expense of the pupils and teaching itself as most of the teachers spent their time filling in forms and reaching targets instead of doing what they signed up for. No wonder stress-related problems affected nine out of ten teachers.

Annie had battled various people in meetings whose faces she wouldn't recognise in the street the next day. She railed against the time taken following, then writing up, these rules and their outcomes. She tried to prove by grade and behaviour statistics and impassioned pleas, that it was all having a detrimental effect on pupils and the whole teaching structure.

It was at the end of the school year this summer, when warned that her constant opposition could mean dismissal by fair means or foul, that she realised she needed to get out. She couldn't seem to reach anyone with her valid grievances and felt like she was wading through treacle. She felt then that she couldn't go back to an institution she no longer respected. She would never make a dent in the plans of the 'faceless ones', their minds were already made up and the meetings were just for show. She handed her notice in a week later. That was the main cause of her flight to a less stressful life but there were others.

She taught art classes three nights a week at her local adult education college and every Saturday morning, she helped out at a 'Kreative Klass for Kiddies'. Their artwork may have improved but she feared for their spelling skills...

She was also having to fit in meetings for committees and sub-committees and she had started doing illustrations in her 'free' time for her friend Lettie's children's books. She would go to bed on a night so tired that sleep wouldn't come. She was past it. It was all her own fault, she realised this. She didn't know why she had this need to push herself but she seemed to be caught in a hamster-wheel that wouldn't stop turning.

After her resignation, in a rare moment of clarity, she realised that it couldn't end there. All the other things had to stop too – a clean break. She thought long and hard about what mattered to her and what she really wanted out of life.

Her happiest times had been staying in holiday cottages in the Yorkshire Dales with her parents when she was young. Meadow Cottage had come up for rent just at the right time for both her and the owners. They wanted everything signed and put into place before they left to visit family in Australia and Annie needed to do this before she could change her mind. She needed a plan, something to hold on to and dispel the uncertainty she felt. Had she done the right thing?

She would miss her pupils – toddlers, children and adults – but the teaching staff changed so regularly that she counted them as acquaintances rather than friends. Her good friend Lettie she would have missed if she hadn't already moved over 200 miles away to Scotland to be with her new husband. Most of their contact now was by email and Zoom.

As for romantic relationships, no one special had ever emerged. She seemed to lurch from one unsuitable relationship to another. She had put up with obsessive jealousy, childish moods and possibly the worst – terminal boredom. Her last boyfriend had come close to hitting her when he was drunk and that's when she decided, at 27, that she was better off on her own. After that, she had stuck to her principles, which now she came to think of it, was maybe why she threw herself into so many different things.

In her new life, she thing she was thoroughly enjoying doing the illustrations, The ink and watercolour depictions of the two mischievous sheepdogs, Millie and Maud, and Lettie's story of their adventures on the farm, had sold very well and had become immensely popular with young children. So much so that they had been commissioned to produce a series which was taking care of Annie's day to day living expenses to an extent. It wasn't a fortune though and would need to be supplemented by other illustrating offers. She wanted to see if she could recapture the 'free spirit' that she had been at art college.

She had rented her own three bedroomed modern house out to a lovely family for a year and that would pay the mortgage and the ridiculously low rent she was paying for Meadow Cottage. She thought that the owners just really wanted someone to look after it until they came back. Annie reckoned they would have paid her to live in it if it was any nearer their leaving date.

Anyway, here she was and at the moment anyway, it seemed like it was the right decision. Was it relaxing? Possibly - but she seemed to have turned from an efficient, intelligent person into a hare-brained, clumsy, foot-in-mouth sort of person who had certainly made an impression on the village since she arrived, even if it wasn't the one she wanted to make.

Yet she could feel that her shoulders had dropped a few inches and there was a permanent half-smile on her face. Most importantly, she could feel her enthusiasm for life returning. She raised her glass, said 'Cheers' to no-one in particular – and her smile widened.

Chapter 6

Mid-December arrived with a prolonged snowfall that showed no sign of relenting. You couldn't tell where the road ended and the pavements began and the snow that had settled on the yews in the churchyard threatened to snap the branches off with the weight.

The surrounding hills looked so picturesque but more so when viewed from behind the window of a room glowing with heat from the fires. The church looked like something off a Christmas card and just needed a robin redbreast on a spade to look authentic. Great big flakes were still twirling and falling onto the white carpet below.

Annie had found a shovel in the garden shed and had cleared the path in front of Bank Farm Terrace, earning her a cup of tea and some malted milk biscuits from Maisie and lots of banter from the other side with Tom's 'You've missed a bit' earning him the threat of a snowball from Annie and a good-natured dig in the ribs from Ada.

Judging by the news on the radio, this weather was set in for the week and she needed supplies. Her cheeks hadn't stopped glowing from her snow-clearing so she thought she might as well go now. She made a shopping list with far too many body-warming carbohydrates and plenty stew and dumpling ingredients as she was in full winter warming food mode. She left space so she could add her neighbour's lists because, despite clearing this short stretch of pavement, there was no way they could walk down to the village. She hadn't seen anyone down the lane, walking or driving and the snow looked pristine - if there were any marks they had been already covered up. She hadn't heard any engine noise from the village either, it was strangely silent all around. She wondered if it was cut off but probably the sound was just muffled in the cushion of deep snow. Only the hardiest of walkers and drivers would be out today – and the foolish and desperate, she smiled, thinking of her sparse store cupboards.

Tom and Ada were very grateful as Tom had just been putting his coat on reluctantly when she knocked. Maybe a large loaf and some tins of soup – and some meat, veg, milk…

Maisie apologised for not wanting to go out and asked for a loaf, tins of beans and peas – and some chops – and 'if it's not too much trouble, a bag of potatoes and some milk.

As Annie went back to fetch her bags she realised that walking back up the hill with all the items on her not inconsiderable list was going to be nigh on impossible.

An idea framed slowly in her head and she crunched her way over to the garden shed again. This time she emerged with a child's sledge which she had noticed earlier, propped at the back, along with some rope hanging on a nail. She gathered up one of the large, heavy-duty boxes from a corner of the kitchen, which she had packed her books in and then set off, more in hope than expectation.

She secured the box on the back of the sledge with some rope and fervently hoping it would stay on when full, set off down the hill, her walking boots getting covered with snow at every giant footstep she took. Unfortunately, the sledge kept bumping into the back of her legs and nearly 'dead-legged' her a couple of times.

She surveyed the pavement, or where the pavement should have been if she could see it and realised it was a straight run down to the bottom of the hill now. It straightened out at the end where the side of the pub was. She looked around but no one was poking their noses outside today, she was alone.

With a grin that might have belonged to her eight-year-old self, she flattened the front end of the box down by stamping on it, mentally reminding herself to put duct tape on the shopping list, and then lowered herself down onto the sledge. This would be so much easier. Grabbing hold of the string at the front, she gave a tentative wiggle up and down. The steep gradient of the hill ensured that this would be enough to set the sledge off at a sedate speed. This didn't last. She was quickly gathering up speed. She belatedly wondered if sledges had brakes as she whizzed down, snow flying out at the front and sides like the wake of the Titanic. She grasped the string, pulling it in case it had any braking properties but then found it laying redundant across her hands, unattached in any way to her improvised bobsleigh.

By this time she had started to panic. The main village through-road was at the bottom. She didn't think of the roads being devoid of cars, her mind just saw a vision of a mangled heap of sledge lodged in the side of a ten-ton truck.

Vaguely, to her left, she caught sight of what could have been the librarian coming out of a door over the lane. An open mouth and a disbelieving expression registered briefly in Annie's mind until she did the only sensible thing left in this situation…covered her eyes.

She heard a man's voice shouting 'Feet. FEET!' and automatically stuck one foot out, making the sledge spin round at a right angle and tip her unceremoniously onto the snow on her back. She blinked up into the eyes of the homeless man turned respectable professor.

'Are you alright?' His deep voice sounded worried.

Annie moved a little and decided the only thing bruised was her pride, although her derriere was coming up a close second, so she nodded. He held out a hand to pull her up while she noticed her resemblance to a yeti. She brushed some snow off as he fought to control his face from showing great amusement instead of the concern he wanted to convey.

She caught a glimpse of faces pushed up against the side window of the pub. There was no sign of Minerva, she'd probably run back in and bolted her door against the madwoman. Annie shivered and surveyed the sledge, still miraculously in one piece. Which was more than could be said for her reputation.

'You look freezing' said the professor, 'can I treat you to a warm meal, if Marje is doing any today that is?' He nodded towards the pub and reaching down for the sledge, pulled it round the corner and straight into the lobby.

Marje turned out to be the pub landlady and it was her and her husband Trevor who had been her audience.

'Best thing I've seen in a long while' wheezed Marje, doubling over, 'certainly brightened my day up. Your face was a picture, you looked like you were headed for the gates of hell.'

'Instead of making directly for me' added the professor, who had stopped fighting the urge to laugh. 'If I hadn't been worried about being used as the jack in a game of bowls, I would have awarded you 9.9 for speed and free expression and minus 2 for control and technique.'

They all collapsed laughing again, Annie included as she was now beginning to see the funny side as she was safe, thawing out and had the prospect of hot food to look forward to.

Trevor brought plates of steaming hot chicken curry, rice and nan bread over to the table nearest the fire. They were the only customers there.

'I reckon you owe Annie this anyway, after she bought you soup and a pot of tea' winked Trevor, obviously not the most tactful person in the village.

'I wasn't going to mention that' apologised the professor as Annie dramatically dropped her head on her arms and whimpered.

'I really, really apologise' she said without looking up, 'it was unforgivable but meant kindly, I promise you.'

'Not at all – and it *was* very kind of you – and I was hungry' This prompted her to look up and he smiled kindly. 'I live a short way up the hill from you but my house is down a private road so it was understandable you thought I was coming from the middle of nowhere. My cold weather clothes are purely to keep me warm. I don't actually give a damn what I look like to others but I think your assessment was understandable.

He had a very gentle smile and the humour reached his eyes, dark brown and intelligent. He was very good looking when you could see his face properly with a sensuous mouth curving up at the corners and dark brown curls framing his face.

'No, I don't care what I look like to others either' she said quickly and not quite truthfully – until she thought of her unscheduled bobsleigh run. 'Obviously' she finished.

'Obviously' he agreed and they both smiled.

'I don't think we've been introduced formally' said the professor, 'I'm Christopher Courtney, usually called Kit by my friends.'

'Does that include me or am I banned from that charmed circle.'

That certainly does include you, I don't buy curries for just anyone you know' he laughed.

'Well Kit, I'm Annie Millford and you can call me Annie because actually I am Annis but I never use it.'

'It's a shame as it's a lovely name - but so is Annie' he added quickly as Annie pulled a face.

'I expect you knew I was Annie Millford before, this being a village?' she grinned

'It was relayed to me by the jungle drums, yes.'

'Yodelling from the hills, pigeon post and now jungle drums. Who needs phones in Winterfell?'

She managed to get all the shopping or alternatives and had asked for duct tape in the 'buy everything here' newsagent. When he knew what it was for, he came out and mended the box with some tape from behind the counter and gave her another, smaller box which would just fit on the front. He helped her rope it all on firmly.

Pulling the full load up the hill on the sledge was easy as it just glided on the runners. It was a lot more dignified than her downwards journey, she reflected ruefully.

DIARY

Well, I've seen it all now. I said before that the new resident Annie acted like a young child. I didn't know how right I was.

I came out of my house today to see the strange spectacle of her tobogganing down the hill at top speed, nearly knocking poor Kit Courtney off his feet before falling off it in a heap. I had to smile though, once I knew she was alright. She may be a little 'off the wall' but she's certainly livening the place up.

I came here five years ago, specifically for a quiet and peaceful life but along with her identifying Kit as homeless, nearly knocking Mr. Cartwright's specs off at the library, that's three times now she's almost made me laugh. I say almost, I don't know why I don't like to laugh or even smile in public. I wasn't popular at the different schools I went to and every time I tried to join in with my fellow pupils' laughter, they stopped laughing and looked at me like I was from another planet. I suppose it stems from that.

My parents were hippies which marked me out as different. They were hippies both before and after it was trendy to be a hippie. Long hair hanging in curtains over their faces, loose flowing garments - my school 'friends' used to laugh and say my father looked like Jesus. They don't know how wrong they were but I wasn't going to put them right.

My parents became involved with a cult and that meant I was involved too. I bided my time until I could get out of the hell holes they took me to. I suppose it wasn't all bad, although the bad bits were VERY bad. I suppose the only things I've learnt from those days are that your parents are most definitely not always right and also that there is nothing wrong with spirituality if it is used and expressed in the right way.

Anyway, as I was saying, this Annie nearly made me laugh out loud, which is saying something. When I found out from Mr. Clegg at the newsagents that she had used the sledge to do some shopping for her neighbours in this shocking weather, it made me wonder whether there is more to her than I first thought. I do make snap decisions which are not always right so maybe I ought to revise my views.

I, of course, went into the library today. I knew no one would want to come to change their books in this weather - and no one did. No one wants to risk life and limb in the snow, especially when most of the people who go there are pensioners. I am paid to do my job though, so I do it. I only live at the bottom of the lane after all and it saves on heating at home. The cat snuggles up in his bed on the window seat and is happy waiting for me there. Besides, what would I do if I didn't go in to work? Read, I suppose. I usually do. I don't 'do' coffee with friends, mostly because I don't have any and no one asks. My own fault, I give off the wrong signals. 'Sulky little B....' my mother used to call me.

More snow is forecast so we might have a white Christmas, not that it will make any difference to me. A chicken dinner on a tray in front of the TV, watching 'It's a Wonderful Life' - and Leofric stretched out on the settee, purring contentedly. Just another normal Christmas for me. It's just one day and then back to normal, thank goodness

Chapter 7

Annie stared across the road at the church. She had just seen a middle-aged couple go through the lych-gate, along the path and up to the porch. She didn't recognise them. Listen to her, she'd been here five minutes and expected to know everyone in the village.

The snow had started to thaw, although more had been forecast. The road was mostly slush but the pavements and paths were quite icy so she had agreed to take Maisie across to the church for the Sunday morning service. She had rashly agreed to stay with her and bring her home as they had both been invited to Tom and Ada's for fruit cake and lemon drizzle cake afterwards.

Annie had told Maisie about her encounter with the vicar and Maisie said that it didn't surprise her in the least, that he wasn't a very nice person but they didn't think he'd been quite well for some time. She said she wouldn't be surprised if he left soon as he never seemed happy and that she hoped he would anyway. So did Annie. She would try and hide behind someone at the back so he didn't see her.

Five minutes now and she would go and collect her neighbour. She thought back to her snowy encounter with Kit. They had a lovely conversation after their meal until Annie realised she had some shopping to do. He talked of his love of pre-history and archaeology and he had written books on the subjects. He travelled to digs and helped them out in an advisory capacity, occasionally spending all his time there if there was one that particularly interested him. He also lectured at the university and gave talks all over the country, although he had scaled that down recently as his writing took over and frankly, he said, he enjoyed his own company more than that of others, and the peace and quiet that writing brought.

She told him about her former job, her busy life and her renouncing of it to try a new career with less stress. She *did* like people in general but was looking forward to having time to herself. They smiled warmly as they realised they were, in essence, aiming for the same thing and they raised a glass to each other. Someone so gorgeous couldn't possibly be so nice, she thought, then shook her head to dispel that thought because a) she shouldn't subscribe to stereotypes and b) she shouldn't be thinking of men in terms of 'gorgeous'. Friends only, was the way to go if she didn't want her new life ruined before it had begun.

The mechanical bells from the church started ringing. Such a shame they weren't actual bells, thought Annie, then realise she had no say in the matter anyway as she didn't go to church. She pulled on her best deep red woollen coat as she didn't want to let Maisie down with her parka, then walked out to collect Maisie. They met Ada and Tom on the pavement.

'I could have taken Maisie you know.' said Tom.

'I do know but Maisie thought I might like to see the church as it's usually locked.' she lied.

'Ah, there is that.' replied Tom, his pride intact.

Annie watched Tom and Ada struggle across the road and thought that they had enough on holding each other up, let alone Maisie. Her heart was in her mouth, she was terrified that any of her lovely neighbours would slip. She had become very fond of them in a short time.

Although Annie wanted to melt into the background as much as possible, Maisie wanted them to sit on the second row in her 'usual' seat.

An elderly woman struck up the organ and they all sang a hymn which luckily Annie remembered the words to from school. The vicar, the Reverend Osbert Wellingport then strode forward to climb to his place at the lectern to survey the congregation which, it had to be said, was very small. He reminded her of Voldemort with a nose. Stop it, she told herself, give the poor man a chance.

As he reached his lofty perch, his eye fell on Annie and his sour expression deepened. His eyebrows went even lower as he scanned the back of the church. His voice fired up, breathing hell and damnation, like a Victorian preacher, over his congregation.

'You sinners!' he shouted.

Woah!, thought Annie, good way to get the community on your side.

'You come before me and before God, purporting to worship Him, yet you keep to your foul pagan ways as your ancestors did. You can't even see you are all cursed for believing in the devil and will go straight to hell! Unless you renounce your wicked ways and come back to the bosom of the church, eternal life will be denied you!'

What is this?, thought Annie, have I walked into a stage set of Jane Eyre here with the Reverend Brocklebank played by Voldemort? This was surreal. Why would anyone come to church to be insulted and abused like this? One look at Maisie's incredulous face and Ada and Tom exchanging horrified glances in front of her told her this wasn't the norm. In fact, as she risked a glance behind her, people were looking puzzled and annoyed. Maybe there was an obscure point to this sermon that they were all missing?

'You!'

She heard the word and then the uncomfortable silence after it before she turned back to the vicar and saw he was pointing at her.

'You – you come into this village and tell me to my face that you don't come to church, that you are a non-believer – an atheist. A scarlet woman in a scarlet coat. You are ripe to join the other devil worshippers in this village. How dare you come into my church and pretend to be something you're not? How dare you use this church for your own means, sneering at those of the true faith?'

Annie stood open-mouthed as all around her there was a collective gasp and then a low murmur, like angry bees. She could feel Maisie's arm curl around hers, squeezing it for reassurance as Ada tutted loudly in front of her. They were still all a little nervous of vicars who, like teachers, still commanded respect. She wasn't though. The man was obviously deranged. A village of devil worshippers? She tried to hold her reaction back. The vicar obviously had a problem, apart from the fact he had been born a couple of hundred years too late. She should just walk out, quickly and quietly. Best thing all round. Obviously the little devil she had been accused of communing with, was sitting on her shoulder whispering as she only made it as far as the aisle before she spoke up.

'I didn't say I was an atheist but whatever I am, my religion or lack of it, is my own affair as this is not *your* church but belongs to the people. I am not a devil worshipper though and neither, I am sure, are the people of this village.'

There was a murmur of assent and a vigorous nodding of heads.

'I may not be religious but I believe that anyone has a right to worship in any way they see fit. There are some people here who will be very upset by your accusations. People who have come to church all their lives.'

She looked across at her neighbours who nodded encouragingly.

'I can't personally refute your words about the village – although I have met with nothing but kindness and goodwill here- but I can say that you have no right to say those things about me.

I am going to throw these words at you. 'Love your neighbour as yourself' You are not following these words of Jesus. Kindness, goodness, forgiveness and understanding is what Christianity is all about. I see precious little of any of this in you.'

Tears started to prick Annie's eyes as she looked at the dumbstruck and red-faced vicar, then before she made even more of a fool of herself, she walked steadily with her head held high, back down the aisle towards freedom. Just before she reached the door, she noticed with a jolt that Kit was seated at the back.

It was only when she got outside and saw the snow that she realised she had a dilemma. She couldn't leave Maisie to negotiate the icy lane by herself. As she grimaced then turned back towards the church, the heavy wooden door flew open and Kit came out. He smiled at her sympathetically and put his arm round her shoulders.

'Well done!' he said warmly and squeezed her again before releasing her as the door opened again.

Maisie, Ada and Tom, accompanied by Marje came through it and behind them, a grey-haired man in tweeds. A younger man then appeared, shoving his white blond hair under a flat cap and holding the elbow of Minerva, the librarian, who Annie had started calling Min in her mind, so she wouldn't seem as scary. Frank the plumber also appeared accompanied by a plump, rosy-cheeked lady on his arm. It was a mass exodus! Annie looked on in horror.

'Please tell me you haven't all deserted because of me?

There were various replies of 'yep' and 'of course' and the main one from Maisie.

'Not just because of you love, although there was no excuse for his treatment of you – but because we have put up with him for too long and you are the only person who had the guts to stand up to him. You've set us free.'

Annie sighed with relief and then tentatively asked,

'I don't suppose any of you would like to tell me what on earth he's on about, would you?'

There were nods of assent although there a was a complicit reluctance between them which intrigued Annie. She thought of her small rented cottage and the limited seating arrangements, which she mentally totted up.

'Would you all like to come over to mine for a drink?' she asked.

Chapter 8

Everybody seemed to be talking at once. Annie watched them and smiled as she searched for drinks and glasses while Marje put the kettle on and searched for cups. Annie found wine, whisky and a pack of beer which she didn't drink but luckily had bought 'just in case'.

Her neighbours had settled themselves down on the comfortable seats in the sitting room along with Frank and his wife Pat. She could hear them chattering away nineteen to the dozen. As she went in to see if they wanted tea or coffee, Tom came back in the front door carrying a tray of small glasses and a bottle of sherry in his voluminous coat pocket. Sherry? Decadence in the extreme, though Annie, smiling to herself.

'Didn't think you'd have this stuff for the ladies' he shouted although he was only a few feet away 'so I've brought ours.'

'Tom Elthwaite, my best glasses! It's a good job you didn't slip on that ice and break them.'

'Notice she didn't worry about me breaking any bones, only her best glasses.' Tom laughed, winking at Frank.

As he poured out a sherry for the ladies, he asked for a small whisky and Frank asked for a beer. So much for a sedate tea or coffee. They all resumed their conversation, talking over each other in a bid to be heard. Annie turned back to the kitchen as gales of laughter erupted from behind her. She grinned - no one would think they'd all been threatened with eternal damnation.

Suddenly, there was a knock at the door and everything went quiet. They all obviously had the same thing on their mind, was it the vicar come to shout at them again at ninety ear-splitting decibels?

The man in tweed stood at the kitchen door in readiness while Kit pushed past her to open the door, his face grim. He seemed to realise that Annie couldn't face another tirade today. On the doorstep stood the fair-haired man from earlier, looking very nervous at this reception.

'I just went to check on Chess first' he stuttered in explanation, 'Is it okay if I join you?'

'Ah' Kit smiled, stepping back to let him in, 'how is she doing?'

71

'Not too badly. Still quite weak of course but rallying a bit now.'

Marje offered an explanation as she opened the bottle of wine. This was apparently Gavin Bradley, the junior vet who worked for the man in tweed- Percy Brindleton-who owned the village veterinary practice. Chess was part of a litter of sheepdogs born to Kit's dog and had been the runt, refusing to eat and consequently nearly died. The drinks were then handed out with the only cup of tea, ironically, going to Marje herself, the pub landlady.

Kit banged the table saying 'The meeting commences' and the noise died down. The ones from the other room joined them and squeezed onto the settle and chairs while the others stood where they could. He addressed them all.

'I thought after being called a scarlet woman' cue much tutting and shaking of heads, 'that Annie here deserved an explanation. So with your permission, I'm going to give her one.'

Cue raucous laughter all round and even louder tutting from the settle, apart from Maisie who just looked puzzled. Kit covered his face with his hands.

'I will ignore your dirty minds and continue' he said, looking engagingly embarrassed and flustered.

'Annie, have you heard of the Winterfell Stone?

She looked confused and shook her head.

'It's a monolith, a standing stone, probably from the early Neolithic era. We are not quite sure of its original purpose but we can make educated guesses. These are guesses for a good reason'

All very interesting thought Annie but…

'The Stone, unfortunately, stands in a local farmer's field which abuts my land. Gardman is his name. If it had been 500 yards further my way, or towards Wentforth's land, we wouldn't have this problem. You see we think that it may have once been the centre stone of a stone circle and has survived intact by virtue of it being much taller and heavier than the others. The others have disappeared from sight over a few thousand years but I think the remains of them are still there, buried under the undulations of the field. There are several small mounds that are crying out to be investigated.

The stones may have been broken up and used as building material in later years but as we have found no evidence of ancient stonework in the village, we think that they might still exist, even if broken, under layers of soil.

In the Sixties, a tentative dig over near the public right of way between the wood and the field, led to evidence of an earlier standing stone made of millstone grit which would have been transported from ten miles away, like the Winterfell stone. This led to the hope of more stones. Gardman's father though, was a religious fanatic, as is his son, The actual information became enhanced, as rumours do and the next thing is Gardman thought a pagan temple was about to be found on his land. He ordered everyone off his land and threatened everyone with the law if they trespassed or disturbed his land in any way. Which is his right, I'm afraid, as he owns the land. There is no right of way across it, only alongside it.'

'So, this is where the vicar's devil-worshipping comes in?' asked Annie, intrigued now. 'Could it be a pagan temple?'

'If we were to find more stones, it is possible that it may have been a place of worship, borne out by the ancient name of the land it stands on, Langstow Rigg, stow originally meaning 'place of assembly'. The name will be from much later but these things are passed down and remembered.

The stone is important to the village. All these people crammed into your cottage today are from a little group formed to get Gardman to change his mind as the authorities are powerless to intervene and believe me, I've tried every

74

authority I could. Including praying to the highest authority. The rest of the village is behind us and attends our little meetings when they can but this is the core group who still attend, even though I rarely have any news for them now.

So, no devil worship at all. Around 5000 years ago, these Neolithic people relied on the weather, they were starting to become farmers and keep animals. They will have gone up to the stone, probably on solstices, or midsummer, Lammas …and worshipped the natural elements. The sun and moon, the earth and water. They were the gods. The Stone is supposed to have mystical qualities even today. Pagan yes but not devil worship. Although there are local legends associated with the Stone which is supposedly magical

I'm afraid I can't tell you any more about it until I, along with my colleagues, can get into that field and examine the place. We don't want to make it a place where people are tramping up there every day, we want to respect the place and get a preservation order on it before Gardman churns everything up with his tractor. I made an unlawful dash to the other side of the Stone last week to get some soil samples from round one of the smaller stones sticking out there. It had been damaged   tractors and small pieces were broken off, I sent a minute piece off to be analysed to give us an idea of age. I know this won't go any further than our little group.

Yet we do want it as a special place for the village. A meeting place at certain times of the year as it was always meant to be. We're very protective of our Winterfell Stone as you can see. It's been a running battle for decades and with my grandfather at Huntingdon Hall before me too. It's so frustrating.'

Kit clenched his fists and scowled and Annie could see just how important this was to him. It was almost a crusade.

'We're all behind him' said the vet, Percy, 'we want to find out our history too. The stone is three-quarters of a mile out of the village and in an isolated position, so there would be no disruption if they dig.'

There was a murmur of agreement which Marje interrupted.

'You know Gardman and the vicar are as thick as thieves don't you? United by their extreme fanaticism? Well, I don't know how many of you are aware that today was Wellingport's last service, which explains why he was more vindictive than usual. Trevor and I got a petition up, complaining about his uncharitable behaviour. Did you know he'd banned Christmas? No carols, family services, nativity, nothing! We sent it to the bishop – I know the churchgoers here signed it- and they sent a representative to one of us for his services. Luckily it was the one where he said we were all sinners, told us off soundly for not giving any more money to the church, (one of the richest bodies in the country), and said that as well as banning carols at Christmas, he wouldn't be using any of the more frivolous hymns either. Anyway, the bishop got back to us and they are having him removed for a respite period in one of their retreats and then will hopefully find him a new position, many miles from here. The arctic circle, hopefully.'

'I doubt if they'll allow him to preach again unless he proves he's changed' said Annie. 'The job has obviously got on top of him and it's just been too much. He looks like he's retirement age so maybe he could just live a quiet life now and recover?'

There was a stunned silence until Frank said

'You're sticking up for him, after all, he said to you?'

'No, he was awful. All I'm saying is that usually, people act in certain ways for a reason, they're not born like it. Perhaps underneath there still remains some of the young boy who was once there. Life attacks us sometimes. Leaving here could be the best thing for him – as well as us.' Annie finished with a shy smile.

She wondered if she'd said too much but she noticed Min smiling over at her and noted that it was the first time she had seen her smile.

'Well Amen to that.' said Marje adding that she had to get back before Trev gave her a sermon worse than Reverend Wellingport's.

'We ought to join together more to fight it and maybe have extra meetings. What do you think Annie, are you with us?' Gavin looked sideways at her and coloured up.

'I am – and I think it's a great idea. Could we use the Meeting Room again Min, m… Minerva?' Oops, she'd called her Min in public but it didn't seem to have been noticed.

'I imagine so. We are a valid group and as such authorised to use the room.' Min replied.

'What do you call yourselves?' Annie asked.

They all looked at each other.

'We don't' answered Min.

There was a short silence interrupted by Maisie.

'We could call ourselves The Stone Circle? You know, like a knitting circle but…different.' She said with a smile.

'Brilliant' said Kit, 'The Stone Circle it is. It's so good to see you all behind this. We need to find a legal way to do this dig or we're sunk. There may, after all this, be nothing there but the indications lead us to believe there are other stones, which could tell us more about the site. So, Annie, we are not devil worshippers. We don't use the stone for pagan worship ...'

Kit paused and glanced across at Min who lowered her eyes.

'...although, like Annie said in church, everyone's faith is their own business and no one else's. '

Odd, thought Annie who had caught the look. Now she watched Marje raise her eyebrows slightly at Min who again suddenly found the kitchen floor very interesting. Hmm, intriguing. There was more to this Stone thing than met the eye.

They all started filing out, laughing and joking as though they had been at a party rather than doing religious penance.

Percy offered to walk Min home so he could check on Leofric, her cat, who had been under the weather. Min looked as pleased as Min ever could and Annie wondered if there was something going on there. Stop it, she thought, you're getting to be a right little village gossip.

Kit very kindly saw Maisie to her door while Gavin hung back.

'Are you going to the ball at Huntingdon Hall on Christmas Eve?' he asked, blushing so the white blond of his hair stood out even more.

'I didn't even know about it, I haven't been invited, is it an Invitation Only do?'

'Well yes but Mr Brindleton and I have been invited as we look after his horses and the other animals, so maybe if you wanted to go…?

He looked so awkward that Annie felt sorry for him but no words would come.

'Could we discuss it over a drink in the Hunter's Moon tomorrow? 7.30 pm? he said, flying out of the door before she could answer him and very nearly running straight into Kit on his way back from Maisie's.

Kit had obviously heard these last words and raised an arched eyebrow, looking very amused. She shut the door. Well, you needn't look so damn pleased about it, she thought, feeling inexplicably annoyed at his reaction.

Diary

Winter Solstice –

Water for purification
Candle for fire
Holly for renewal and new growth.

The Arwen symbol is drawn – three lines
representing the realms of land and sky,
below and above.

We swear by peace and love to stand
Heart-to-heart and hand to hand
Mark, O spirit, hear us now
Confirming this our sacred vow.

May the solstice and the turning of the
wheel bring love, peace and good fortune
in the coming year. We welcome the
returning sun with hope and joy.

Chapter 9

Strange, thought Annie before yawning then gulping her coffee down to wake her up.

It was early morning and the light had not long begun to appear reluctantly over Winterfell. The sun hovered over the horizon and the peach-coloured clouds were tinged with mauve as they tumbled out of a still inky-black sky above them.

She had dragged herself out of bed and into the study as today was the deadline for the Millie and Maud illustrations and she still had one to finish off. Making a coffee, she had taken it up to her work desk to switch the lamp on. As she was doing so, she just glanced out of the window and saw a figure look up at the window in surprise, probably startled by the light.

It was hard to tell because of the cloak the figure wore with the hood pulled down over their face but Annie could have sworn it was Minerva.

What was she doing coming from further up the lane, there was only Kit's house up there wasn't there?

Annie frowned, surely not? Min was about twenty years older than Kit to start with. She shook her head and reminded herself it was none of her business.

Trying to concentrate on the work on her desk, she got everything ready. She checked the 'Glorious Gardens' calendar hanging on the wall behind the desk and there, on the December 21st square and underlined in red was the note 'Deadline for last M&M pic -12 noon' She would make it and just hoped everything was to the publisher's satisfaction. The number of preliminary sketches, the amount of planning and the sheer amount of drawings she had to go through before everyone was satisfied, let alone the emails pinging back and forth would surprise anyone who thought it was an easy job. Although, it was much better than her life at Cambersea.

Before she fetched a jar of water from the bathroom, something niggled at her. She stared again at the calendar. Winter Solstice, it announced in small printed letters under her red felt tip line.

Winter solstice. The Winterfell Stone. Minerva's long cloak and hood. Her furtive glance at the window.

Minerva was a witch! For some reason she found this ridiculously funny and doubled up in silent laughter. This is why secret looks were exchanged between her and Kit, although she would hardly call being a witch a 'faith' but what did she know? She must pass his house going towards the Stone and he must know, or guess what she was going for. Marje the landlady had given her a funny look too, so she must suspect. Annie supposed it wasn't something Min wanted spread around the village. She could just see the headlines in the local paper now.

'STAID AND FRUMPY LIBRARIAN SWAPS HER GREY SUIT AND CONDESCENDING EXPRESSION FOR A LONG CLOAK, WHICH SHE THROWS OFF TO PRANCE NAKED AROUND LOCAL DEVIL'S STONE.'

Okay the last bit was an image too far but Annie giggled to herself at the picture in her mind. Min had agreed the stone wasn't for devil worship so perhaps it was for spiritual matters – a white witch maybe?

Annie was a great believer in live and let live and thought that everyone should do what they wanted if it didn't hurt them or anyone else. She still found it funny though. A more serious thought occurred. Min must be worried now as not only did she realise that Annie had seen her this morning but she would have thought there was a good chance that she had also caught the look between Kit and Min at the impromptu meeting. Would her secret be out?

Min didn't know her well enough yet, so wouldn't know that Annie would never betray anyone like that. She would have to reassure her, if this was the case, that it wouldn't go any further and her lips were sealed. How to approach it though? She couldn't just come out with it. With other people perhaps but not with Min. She would go and choose a few books later and ask her over for coffee. In that way, Min might even broach the subject herself.

She finished the painting of Millie and Maud sitting up, apparently with wide grins on both their faces the way only sheepdogs can, then waited for the last bits to dry. She scanned it and then sent it by email at exactly 11.50 a.m., crossing her fingers while pressing send.

She hoped that her friend would be pleased too. Lettie had invited her up to Scotland for Christmas and New Year but Ada and Tom had already invited her for Christmas dinner, Maisie would be there too. She had accepted as it was so kind of them and she felt she shouldn't abandon the village the first chance she got. Also, she didn't want to outstay her welcome at Lettie's. New Year was on the cards though, they really knew how to celebrate that in Scotland.

Christmas, or Christmas Eve in Cambersea was normally a visit to the pub with her colleagues and then back to hers for an early night. It did seem boring now she thought about it but she was happy enough. This year would be different as she had agreed to go to the Christmas Eve ball at Huntingdon Hall with Gavin.

She had full intentions of making excuses but as she drank her half a cider in the pub with him last night and listened to him talk, she realised that it wasn't her devastatingly gorgeous looks that had prompted him to invite her but that she was the only available person near his age who he could ask. Not that he had told her this, he was far too polite and would be upset if he knew her thoughts but as he spent half the night talking about the younger daughter of the Huntingdon Hall family. The Wentforths, it quickly became obvious where his heart really belonged.

Wendy Wentforth (yes, really…) was apparently blonde, slim and wonderful. She had personally told him all about the ball and Gavin rather naively thought this meant they were going together as a first date. Then she had inexplicably announced, rather sniffily, two days later that she was going with Ashton Delamare whose parents owned the restaurant in the next village.

He was still licking his wounds when Percy had murmured that perhaps he had missed his chance because he couldn't see a hint even if it jumped up and gave him a black eye.

It seemed to Annie that Wendy was trying to galvanise him into action or make him jealous. Unfortunately this passed Gavin by who, besides looking like an overgrown schoolboy with his blond quiff and rosy cheeks, actually had the innocence of said schoolboy. It was obvious to Annie that he just wanted someone to take to the ball to get within worshipping distance of his beloved.

This was why Annie had agreed to go with him - as friends she had stipulated. If Gavin at twenty-seven years old had actually taken a shine to her even though she was all of four years older than him, she would have found some excuse not to go. She loved his innocence and didn't want to let him down. What harm could it do? So now she had to decide what to wear. She had only brought one 'posh' dress which she had never worn but just liked the look of. It was two years old and it might not even fit her any more. It would have to do though.

Now for a quick sandwich for lunch and on to see Min.

*

Annie's happy smile as she walked into the library soon faltered as Min glanced up at her and then pointedly looked away. She chose a few books from the Nature section and took them over to the counter.

'Hi' she said brightly.

Min took the books from her, unsmiling. The library was still the old-fashioned type and hadn't got the do-it-yourself electronic checkout so Min stamped the books very loudly, the sound echoing around them. As she picked the third book up and held it open, Annie coughed lightly.

'I wondered if you'd like to come round for coffee and a chat sometime?' she asked weakly.

There was a different type of stamping noise and a wince from Min as Annie saw she had stamped the back of her own hand. Annie struggled not to smile. Stamping the book now with renewed venom, she passed them over.

'No thank you.' she said.

'Oh' exclaimed Annie, taken aback. She had been expecting an excuse but that was just plain rude. Although at least she said thank you. As there was nothing more to be said she turned to go out, passing Mr Cartwright on the way, who stepped aside to avoid her even though she was nowhere near the door.

She could hear the conversation behind her as she held the door open to go out.

Mr Cartwright: Can I ask if..

Min: WHAT?

Mr Cartwright (whimpering): Well, I just wondered if…

Min: OH FOR HEAVEN'S SAKE!

Annie missed what happened next when the door closed behind her but one result of that conversation might be that on any future visits to the library, Mr Cartwright might come kitted out in full body armour and helmet, with a stun gun in his holster.

Well, thought Annie, she seemed to have handled that wrong. The librarian was irascible but she wasn't a lost cause. As with the ranting reverend, she believed that there was a reason for what appeared to be difficult behaviour.

Chapter 10

Putting on her boots again in her hallway, she
hesitated, then headed back outside. As the cold
air hit her anew, she took backward steps to
release her thick scarf from inside her coat and
use it as a muffler around her lower face,
wondering with an embarrassed blush if anyone
would mistake *her* for a tramp.

She turned left to go up the lane. This standing
stone appeared to be very important to Min and
indeed to the other villagers. It was about time she
had a look at it. The cold was biting into her
cheeks. The snow which had been forecast hadn't
arrived yet but it was bitterly cold. The snow on
the ground mostly remained in the shadier places
but as there was no footpath after Ada and Tom's,
she found herself walking on a still snowy grass
verge.

She found the entrance to the private road, which was a narrow single-track, dirt road which anyone would struggle to get a vehicle up because of the ruts and bumps. It was really only a footpath which Tom had told her joined up with another from the village. There was a house a little way down the lane on her right which announced on a boulder at the entrance, 'Hunter's Lodge'. She had been told a few people Kit knew from this end of the village used it to walk their dogs here, she had reservations about it. She wondered if she ought to go and ask permission at the house but that seemed like an invasion of privacy in itself. She stopped in front of what looked like an early Victorian rectory in part, with an older building behind the façade. The mellow ochre-coloured stone matched that of Meadow Cottage but was cut in larger blocks. There were lots of different aspects to it; one wing to the left had a gable end , then the larger part of the building directly in front of her had a smaller gable end at the right. The slate roof swooped and dipped at angles. On the left wing was a French door and there was a large bay window downstairs on the main part. It seemed to go a long way back and the garden at the front was sizeable too, mostly laid to lawn with hedges and borders which would probably be very pretty in summer. As the house was well set back in the garden, it afforded him privacy from anyone who was walking their dogs and Annie could see it would be a lovely, tranquil place for Kit to write.

As she stood debating what to do, a sudden cacophonous noise erupted into the peace of the day. From the door next to the bay window shot two sheepdogs who flew towards her, sounding quite fierce until they reached the gate and the tone changed to 'now we've scared the life out of you, you can make a fuss of us' sort of whine. She looked up to see Kit leaning against the door jamb with a mug in his hand, looking very amused.

'They're all bark and no bite' he shouted 'but I don't let that be generally known in case of unwanted visitors.'

'Am I one?' she shouted back.

'Not at all.' he laughed.

Annie couldn't help but notice he looked tall, lean and tidy. His hair was pushed back instead of falling about his face in disarray. As he walked towards her she noticed he had a five o'clock shadow but he had the sort of skin which would produce it a few hours after shaving. Testosterone, as well, she thought rather uncomfortably. His white baggy shirt was tucked into a pair of black trousers but the eccentricity still appeared in the form of coloured braces holding the trousers up. She bent down to stroke the eager dogs who vied for her attention.

'Your very own Millie and Maud' She laughed as she saw his puzzled look 'A story for another time'

'I'll look forward to it.' he nodded towards the dogs, 'they're trying to tell me to take them for a walk. Were you coming here?'

Actually, I was wondering if it would be alright if I went and had a look at the Winterfell Stone, so I know what everyone is talking about. It's up here somewhere isn't it?

'Any reason you chose today' he asked, his mug halfway to his lips.

'Yes, I'm aware it's the Winter Solstice' Annie laughed 'although my interest was piqued by seeing Min–erva pass by my cottage early this morning from this direction'

She let her voice trail off and he looked at her for a moment before obviously coming to a decision.

'Not my story to tell' he smiled and changed tack. 'Do you know the way? It's only just over half a mile or so from my house. Straight along here as far as the wood then take the path to the right- the other is an overgrown path leading to the village – skirt round the wood until you see the field on your right and you're facing straight ahead again. The field on the right there is Gardman's, the land up to the wood is mine. Now you'll see the Stone on your right. You won't be able to miss it. You won't be able to go off the public right of way in case Gardman is lurking. How he thinks an ancient stone can *belong* to him, I have no idea – but we don't want to give him any rope to hang us with.'

'So I can't actually get up close to the Stone?'

'You can see it from the wood but you can't get close. I – and others' Did he meant Min? 'have risked going up to it and I have scuttled over the land quickly – but I didn't tell you that'

He looked sternly at her but his eyes were laughing.

'Just a word of warning – Gardman might know it's a solstice and be on the lookout.'

She thanked him and set off at a brisk a pace as the ground would allow. The fast pace didn't seem to be warming her. Following Kit's directions she saw the wood – an ancient wood full of native trees – the ground rose upwards in a gradual incline and she followed the curve of the path until she straightened up again. There she saw it, standing in splendid isolation at the crest of a hill plateau. Although if Kit was right, it was never meant to be isolated but surrounded by other stones. As she walked along, she could see the mounds and bumps in the field that Kit had mentioned before. No wonder the farmer could only use it for grazing although they were worried about his tractor doing damage to the stones so he must cut it occasionally. For hay or to encourage growth perhaps, she acknowledged she was no expert in country life.

She was now directly opposite the Stone. Silvery white brushed the land around it making the dark millstone grit stand out more. Annie could see exactly why people had chosen this as their place of worship or gathering-place. She took a few tentative steps forward away from the wood so that she could see more of her surroundings. The wood may have been ancient but it was almost certainly not here when the Stone was erected. Trees could live to 1000 years or more and some varieties even longer but the chances are this was open land, with the stone central to it and would have been seen for miles around. A potent symbol of power to those living further down in the dale where they would have had a stream and shelter. To come here would have meant a pilgrimage of sorts, to a place that held a special meaning to early man. As indeed it did to this village in the present day reflected Annie.

Annie stared at the Stone; she couldn't tear her eyes from it. She wanted to touch it. It was like a primitive need. Looking quickly all around her and listening for the sound of a tractor, she made a split- second decision. If Min could do it, so could she. 'Go for it', she whispered to herself she ran over the solid ground of the field. Stopping almost within touching distance of the stone, she panted and looked around again.

She was aware as it rose above her, of how much bigger- over twice her height- and how much more presence the Stone had when you were near to it. It was an irregular shape at the top, as though it had been worn away or chipped off. The earth rose up at its base as though some of the stone were buried underneath it and other small stones nearby pushed through the earth.

A watery sun suddenly made an appearance, its light catching the Winterfell Stone, showing its pitted surface. What was it about these stones that stirred the emotions and made the heart beat a little faster? She was a common-sense person but at this moment she could understand Min a little better. It was as though they spoke through the ages to you, personally.

She could feel something drawing her in, making it imperative that she touched it. Her arm reached out, her fingers tingling. She took a step forward.

Suddenly, she heard a voice in the distance. Like a rabbit caught in the headlights, she stood stock still until she slowly let her breath out and turned towards the wood, her head down, ready for flight. Her heart was beating hard again but this time due to an imminent confrontation with The Angry Farmer. She imagined him with a pitchfork in one hand and a scythe in the other, come to exact his awful revenge on her for the sin of trespass. She started to run like a bat out of hell until, as she neared the wood, she heard a sort of cough from where she was making for and stopped dead. Her eyes must have been standing out like chapel hat pegs. Then she heard a bark – no, two different excited barks and peered amongst the trees at the edge of the wood. She could make out a figure with a long coat and a brimmed hat, who was doubled up with laughter. Kit! She ran up to him, not knowing whether to be annoyed or relieved but slapped his arm forcefully anyway

'Did you do that on purpose?' she demanded.

'Of course not' Kit replied still with a stupid grin on his face that he couldn't wipe off even though it might mean another arm slap. 'I told you I had to walk the dogs. I didn't mean to scare you and I didn't mean to laugh either but it was just your face.'

'Thank you.' she growled ironically as he doubled over again.

'You looked like you had the hell-hounds of Lucifer behind you.'

'I thought I had, personified by Farmer Gardman' she said, annoyingly she was starting to smile herself.

'Sorry' he said and squeezed her shoulder.

'It's alright. I suppose it would look funny to an evil sadist…'

He laughed again, then becoming more serious, pointed over at the Stone.

'What did you think?'

'Magnificent' she didn't mention the feelings it evoked, 'I'd love to know how far below the ground it goes and if there is a stone circle surrounding it under those mounds.'

'Join the club then and if you come up with any bright ideas of how we can achieve that let me know. Did you – feel anything?'

Until I know you better Kit Courtney, I'm keeping schtum in case you laugh at me again, she thought and just said. 'Yes, I felt a complete fool breaking the Olympic record for cowardice.'

Kit grinned at her again and this time she joined him.

Diary

I'm so annoyed at that woman, Annie Millford or whatever her stupid name is. I know she saw me returning from the Stone, being nosy from up in her bedroom window. Can't leave some folks alone. Next I knew she was across the road to the library, dying to know more. I wasn't going to give her the satisfaction though.

Then she had the cheek to ask me for coffee and a 'chat'. I know exactly what she wanted to chat about. She pretends she's being nice when instead she's just being patronising. Let's be kind to the local weirdo. Except she's got plenty choice in this village.

Just when I was getting to like her too. She seemed to be quite understanding at the 'gathering' at her cottage - saying that people are usually how they are for certain reasons and we weren't born like it. I can identify.

Then again you see, she's only just arrived and she has everyone eating out of her hand. Some people have it so easy; they drift through life with everything handed to them on a plate while some of us struggle to make ends meet with actual work. Children's book illustrator? Pah! What - an hour a day and then swanning about for the rest of it?

She's invited to the Xmas Eve ball too of course. I've been here five years and I haven't had a sniff of an invite. Not that I'd go even if I was asked. Mr

Brindleton the vet doesn't go either. Not the sort. Very sensible if you ask me.

Oh who am I KIDDING? I don't hate the woman at all - or even dislike her. In fact, I might even like her given the chance. I wouldn't say I'm envious of her exactly but she has it easy in the personality, looks, popularity and life stakes. I bet Percy Brindleton admires her too, although he is not one to have his head turned and did talk more to me and Maisie than the unstinting hostess.

She is, at least, trying to help restore the Winterfell Stone to the village, as are we all. Which is something in her favour, I suppose. I wonder if she really knows why it is so important to me?

Chapter 11

The threatened snow was still holding off this morning, which was just as well because Annie had accepted a lift to the next dale, Ashburndale, over the top of the hills above her.

Marje was picking up a painting of the Hunter's Moon pub she had commissioned for a Christmas present for Trev. Annie suddenly realised she hadn't bought any presents for her neighbours, however small, to say thank you for welcoming her to the village. She was also, weather allowing, going up to Scotland for New Year to Lettie's, so she would need to take her and her husband presents, as well as one for their adorable two-year old, Hamish.

The place she was going to was a courtyard full of cottage craft workshops and Marje was sure Annie would find something to buy there if she wanted a lift. Apart from the high pass between the two dales, the roads were supposed to be fairly clear. Annie had her doubts but according to Trev, his wife was a fearless driver so she had said yes, she would love a lift there.

She sipped her boiling hot cup of tea as though it would insulate her insides and thought about yesterday. After Kit had stopped laughing at her and she had stopped herself thinking what a lovely, happy smile he had..., they had walked back with the dogs Bessie and her daughter Bella. He had told her a bit more of the prehistoric history of the area and that his family were the original owners of Huntingdon Hall. Huntingdon being the name of the original Earldom and Courtney the family name. Family fortunes had dwindled over the centuries and Kit's grandfather had sold the Hall to the 'nouveau riche' Wentforths and their son still lived there, being the father of Wendy, his youngest daughter. The Courtneys had moved into the Gatehouse, Hunter's Lodge, where Kit still lived.

She had a tantalisingly close look inside as Kit lent her a book about standing stones in the Yorkshire area. The study, as he fetched the book from its glass-fronted, craftsman-made wooden bookcases, had been filled with period furniture, probably brought with them from the Hall.

Two large leather, wing-backed chairs stood at either side of a fireplace which dominated the room and had a carved wooden surround of huntsmen and hounds. Under a window stood an enormous leather-covered desk where he probably wrote his books and wrote up his lecture notes. The top of it was almost buried by sundry pieces of paper and piles of text books. The whole room was lined with bookshelves so the study probably did double duty as a library. As he handed the book over she saw the author was one Christopher Courtney. She looked up at him quizzically and he grinned back at her in a self-effacing way.

She had been escorted off the premises by the dogs who probably thought she was taking them for another walk. Her family had always had sheepdogs or border collies as they had called them, so she felt at home with the breed. The most intelligent of dogs she had found, if a little over enthusiastic. In fact, that's where the idea for the 'Millie and Maud' books had come from when she suggested it to Lettie for her stories. Annie loved them but hadn't had the time to devote to a dog since she flew the nest and didn't think it would be fair on a dog if she had one.

The little dog that Gavin was looking after was Bessie's daughter and Bella's sister. Kit hadn't wanted to take Bella on but as the farmer in the next dale had only wanted the two male dogs, Bella and Chess were left. Kit agreed to take Bella but drew the line at Chess. He told Annie he felt bad about it but he didn't have the time to devote to a dog who needed a lot of looking after , possibly for a long while. Gavin agreed to look after her , with Kit paying expenses, until she got better and a home could be found for her.

Her thoughts were interrupted by a car horn that sounded like an elephant in pain. She grabbed her coat and rucksack and closed the front door behind her. She turned round to see an ancient pick-up, covered in mud, with dents and rust holes all over it. She swallowed hard, did the dents and 'fearless driver' marry up? Was fearless a euphemism for 'drives like a maniac'? Hopefully the dents were done by other people.

Marje must have seen her uncertain expression and hastened to reassure her that 'it was a good workhorse that wouldn't let them down. Bull bars on the front in case of snowdrifts or other obstructions.'

Annie had to admit that this didn't help to instil confidence. Especially as Marje set off from standing to 60 mph , hurtling out of the village at a pace more suited to Brand's Hatch than a road with snow still piled at the sides. She thought that the forty-minute journey might prove to be only twenty at this rate. Her legs were already cramping due to pushing imaginary brakes down to the floor.

*

It did prove to be forty minutes by the time they approached the village but only because even Marje had to slow down considerably to go over the tops, which was still covered in snow, quite thickly in places. Annie's eyes had been tightly shut, fingers grasping each side of her seat as Marje chattered about a new menu they were introducing after Christmas, whilst slithering from one side to the other of the narrow road, apparently without a care in the world. She could see where the 'fearless' epithet came in.

Now though, the sign BRYTHERSTONE welcomed them into this part of the Yorkshire Dales. Just after the sign, Marje turned off down a lane signposted 'Mab's Court' and Annie finally relaxed, shoulders coming down four inches back to their normal position. Marje turned right again and parked in a small car park which was surprisingly full of cars. The courtyard itself had lots of people milling about and Annie thought that some must have walked up from the village too.

'Coffee!' sighed Marje and made for a unit in the corner with tables outside. The two inside were taken up so they took their steaming mugs and two huge slabs of gingerbread outside where, although still cold, at least it was sheltered. Marje went off afterwards to see the artist in his workshop while Annie wandered around.

She bought two lovely handmade aprons for Maisie and Ada as they seemed to wear them all the time indoors, and a hand-knitted scarf for Tom, along with some home-made fudge for them all from the bakers. She also bought six leather bookmarks for emergency presents. In a shop full of wooden hand-made objects, a young couple and their children crammed behind the worktable. The woman was heavily pregnant and definitely the earth mother type. The children smiled shyly at Annie and she smiled back warmly. Annie's eyes went straight to a heavy wooden paperweight in the shape of an acorn and mounted on a wooden weighted plinth. Perfect for Kit to keep at least some of the papers on his desk in order. It was a bit more than she wanted to pay for a token present but it was worth it.

She ran back across to the café and bought a coffee and walnut cake that Marje had been salivating over earlier, to say thank you for the lift.

In the herb shop, she bought a box of culinary herbs for Angus, Lettie's husband, who was a brilliant cook. The herb shop's owner, Sadie, asked if the roads were okay as she was hoping for a last push on Christmas gifts here in Mab's Court and was keeping her fingers crossed that the snow stayed away.

A beautiful necklace with bright blue stones was then purchased for Lettie and she went back to the wood shop to buy a wooden train with chunky, removable people, which Hamish would love. When the weather was better, she would definitely visit this place again.

Who else? She wandered across to a stained-glass unit and saw some light catchers hanging in the window. One had a black cat on it, looking very supercilious and wise. Min perhaps? She was drawn for some reason, to one with three cats on: one black, one tabby and one marmalade. She turned to see Marje rushing across the courtyard with a man who was carrying the large painting, which had been very well wrapped up. 'Five minutes' Marje signalled by showing 5 digits and Annie replied by sticking her thumb up.

Annie decided to take the chance on the three cats and hurriedly bought it before racing back to the truck.

The journey back didn't seem quite as bad or maybe Annie was just getting used to Marje's driving.

'Brilliant painting he's done' said Marje 'Wish I could show you it but he's wrapped it up in so many layers it looks like a particularly awkward 'pass the parcel' game. Can you give me a hand to get it past eagle eyes? I'll go in the back way. If he comes out from behind the bar, distract him.'

Trev had no idea what he was getting but where you could hide four feet by three feet object from him, Annie had no idea.

'Under the bed in the spare double bedroom' Marje said suddenly as Annie squeaked in surprise. Could she read her mind? 'That's where I'll put it.'

Well, maybe not then but still, Annie kept giving her sneaky glances all the way home to see if she came out with anything else. In case she could read minds, she tried not to think of anything she shouldn't – which immediately made her think of everything she shouldn't.

When she had helped Marje with the painting, given her the cake and thanked her profusely, she picked up a few things from the shops and went home. As she went up the hill she realised it *was* home. The range would be keeping the place warm to welcome her. At the door, she looked up the lane. The sky was heavy and deep purple, edged with pink. Then the first snowflakes started to fall.

Chapter 12

Throughout the night, the snow had fallen continuously and it was still coming down in huge flakes.

The Christmas Eve ball tonight would have been cancelled apart from the fact that they had already bought all the food in and preparations were already underway. The snow was so deep that only those with four-track vehicles would be able to reach Huntingdon Hall although there were rumours of tractors being sent with trailers on the back, equipped with cushions - ideal for someone going to the ball in their finery! Some brave souls, not wanting to miss the local social event of the year would no doubt trudge up from the village and along the extremely long driveway in the bitter cold.

Word had got around that Eddie from the estate farm had used the snow plough attachment on his tractor and cleared the driveway as much as possible but as almost blizzard conditions prevailed, it would be like...shovelling snow in a blizzard!

Many of the guests were well-to-do acquaintances of the Wentforths and would be cut off from the village. Quite a few though had been house guests for the last couple of days and had filled up all the many bedrooms in the Hall so the event wouldn't be as much of a failure as it could have been. They were staying on for a private Christmas and Boxing Day party there.

Gavin had rung Annie to say it would still be alright for them to go as his four- track was used to reach the most inhospitable places in all weathers but to bring her wellies and a thick coat just in case. They were giving a lift to two other couples from the village too, if she didn't mind? Of course Annie didn't mind but she really didn't want to go. If it wasn't for trying to further love's young dream, she wouldn't bother. She looked longingly at the red glow of the range and the warm lamps making her kitchen so cosy and sighed. It was time for her to get ready.

She had only brought one 'posh frock' with her and she looked at it now as she stood in front of the mirror. She must have put on a little weight since she tried it on as it seemed a snugger fit, following her shape closely but she was still quite pleased at the effect. Her dirty blonde curls necessitated a stronger colour in the dress or she would just look washed out. So she had gone for a heavy silver satin overlaid with a midnight blue lace. The overall effect was dark blue but with the silver showing through, catching the light and shimmering as she walked.

Smiling to herself, she thought the dress would go beautifully with the thick black leggings and the battered walking boots she was wearing underneath and with the long 'scarlet woman' coat and the green woolly hat she was wearing to top the ensemble off. Looks didn't matter in this weather.

Annie grinned, remembering her teenage years when she would wear a thin, short dress and three-inch heeled strappy sandals to go out in the depths of winter. Coats and sensible shoes weren't cool then. Now, she just wanted to be warm. Depending how warm it was at the Hall, the leggings might stay on under the dress too. She slipped her dark blue, heeled court shoes into her rucksack and would change when she got there.

She had tried putting her hair up in an elegant style but ended up looking like a poodle being shown at Crufts. Instead, she found a large silver barrette in her jewellery box and had just pushed her hair back on one side with it.

She could hear a scrunching noise in the muffled hush of the snow-filled night. She went to the window and saw headlights lighting up a white expanse. This would be Gavin as it was the only car she had seen up here all day.

She locked up and climbed into the passenger seat after greeting the two couples squeezed in the back, who she had never seen before. Gavin seemed quite happy driving in these conditions although he probably would have driven through far worse conditions than this just to be able to exchange a few words with the wonderful Wendy Wentforth. He turned the car round in Kit's driveway and after a slow but surprisingly steady journey they arrived at the Hall, which was lit up in every window like the battery-operated pottery houses you see in garden centres at Christmas.

Gavin dropped them at the door and went off to the left to park as the other couples headed inside, enticed by the warmth and the music. Annie thought it was only polite to wait for Gavin though so she stood to the side of the steps, stamping and hugging her arms round her body to keep warm.

As she stood there, she noticed a figure strolling towards the Hall down the driveway. She would recognise it anywhere. Kit had his ankle-skimming, voluminous wool coat on, which made him seem even taller than he actually was, which was tall! The collar was pulled right up and the leather fedora, now with a layer of snow, sat on his head. A scarf was wound many times around his neck up to his ears and only his eyes were visible. This time he reminded her of a cowboy in one of those gritty Westerns, walking down the main street, ready to draw his guns on anyone who annoyed him. His long strides soon brought him up to the door.

'Well hello, fancy meeting you here' he smiled, 'I recognised you from back there in that coat – are you on Scarlet Woman duties tonight then?'

'I'm not going to dignify that with an answer' she replied.

'Is Gavin around?'

'Just gone to park the car and before you make a glib remark, I'm definitely not on Scarlet Woman duties with him. He needed a partner quickly and I'm a soft touch.'

'Well come inside while you wait then, it's freezing out here.' He grabbed her arm and ushered her into the large round hallway, which displayed a twelve-foot decorated Christmas tree and had white columns around the outside, each gap leading to a different room or passageway. He pointed to a room off a passage to the right.'

'Ladies cloakroom there. I'm a big fan of the big lace-up boots with evening wear but…'

'I have my glass slippers in here' and she held up the rucksack, which luckily contained an evening purse too.

'Then you *shall* go to the ball Cinders, just as long as your prince hasn't pranged the pumpkin parking it.'

Annie laughed as she headed off to divest herself of her multi-layers. It was warm enough in here to take her leggings off too – for now. She handed everything over to a young girl who hung up her coat and stored her bag and boots neatly underneath. With one last look in the mirror after re-doing her hair, she went out into the hallway to find Gavin. He was deep in conversation with a portly man with shoulders that reminded Annie of a 1930s gangster. She stood back and waited, not wanting to interrupt.

She became aware of Kit before she saw him. She could feel his eyes burning into her. Slowly she turned towards him. Divested of his cowboy coat he looked, it had to be said, devastatingly handsome. He was wearing a tuxedo which completely shook the eccentric Poldark look off and presented a tall, slim and elegant figure. His dark brown curls were still escaping over his face but that only added to the charm. Taller than those around him, he stood out and Annie couldn't take her eyes off him. Obviously Kit felt the same, as all through her appraisal he had been staring at her. He started to walk over to her and she felt ridiculously nervous. He laid one hand on the top of her arm and stroked it gently.

'You look beautiful' he said in a low voice.

'You don't look so bad yourself' whispered Annie, looking straight into those deep brown eyes. How long they stayed like this she couldn't remember but they were interrupted by Gavin, rushing up to them and totally unaware of any undercurrents.

'Sorry Annie, just talking to Alfred about a pig. Distended gut probably. Hi Kit' and with that, Gavin herded her into the ballroom.

Annie gasped as she entered the room. It was predominantly decorated in cream and gold with elaborate cornicing all around the ceiling, containing mouldings of cherubs, stags and trees. There were three huge ceiling roses painted gold with elaborate crystal chandeliers hanging down low from each one, all of them ablaze with light. Small round tables had been placed around the outer edges of the floor and white and gold chairs were placed around them. In the gaps between each table were console tables containing displays of flowers in white and gold with twigs of red berries adding that extra touch. In each corner was a pedestal with a jardiniere overflowing with a display of white and gold flowers, trailing almost to the floor. Apart from the large entrance door she had just walked through, there was a door leading off on the far wall. Large arched windows looked out onto the driveway where more snow could be seen flying past diagonally.

The people sitting at the tables, no one was dancing as yet, were all dressed in their finery. This was obviously the event of the year in normal circumstances and Annie was surprised to see how many had actually made it. She imagined that it was usually crammed so full that you couldn't move. She actually preferred it like this, although the ball was for charity, so for the Wentforths, she supposed the more people who came, the better.

The music, coming from a band on the dais in the far corner, changed from gentle background music to louder dance music. A few people got up onto the floor and started dancing, holding each other close. Gavin looked at her and she looked back at Gavin and there was a tacit agreement between them they wouldn't be joining them.

Chapter 13

The ball itself was disappointing, not least to the Wentforths who must have spent a considerable time planning this only to be scuppered by the weather. The money for all the tickets that had been sold had been donated anyway by those who couldn't get here, so the charity itself wouldn't suffer.

It was mostly disappointing to Annie though because Kit had come here, not on his own as she had thought but to partner Wendy's older sister, Isolde, who stood in the Circle of Hell looking like the cat who'd got the cream. The Circle of Hell, christened by Annie, being a group of people all standing round looking like they'd rather be anywhere but stuck with this particular circle.

Isolde, dark and beautiful (despite her angular face, too long nose and pinched mouth, thought Annie ungenerously) was the only one who looked happy with her lot, gazing up at Kit in adoration. Annie thought she recognised the look as being less of adoration and more of possession, as in 'he's mine so nobody go near' but thought this might be ungenerous too. Although why it bothered Annie, she didn't know. She was just friends with Kit and nothing else had been intimated. Calm down dear, she thought to herself.

Kit, next to her, looked gratifyingly bored, staring at a fixed point over everyone's heads and being uncharacteristically quiet. On his left was Wendy, who tried to maintain an imperious expression but ruined it by anxious sidelong glances at Gavin every thirty seconds. Ashton, her partner for the evening, was looking uncomfortable – as well he should with his touch of mascara and his furtive glances at one of the young men going round with a tray of drinks. He'd obviously been railroaded into this and you could drive a two-ton truck in the gap between himself and Wendy, both physically and metaphorically.

Annie sympathised with him as she was here for the same reason. She hadn't let him know she was doing him a favour so perhaps Gavin felt obliged to stick with her but she just wished he'd get on with it and actually talk to Wendy and then she could escape the Circle of Hell. Apart from the occasional realisation that Annie was here when he blinked, smiled and said 'Isn't this nice?' or Can I get you a drink?', he had spent the entire evening staring at Wendy like a lovesick puppy. For that reason, Annie stuck it out and smiled to herself at his obvious devotion to the lovely Wendy, the love of his life.

The group broke apart thankfully, when the dancing began again after a short break. The music sounded slightly discordant to Annie's ears as a couple of the ensemble who hadn't been staying here, hadn't made it through the snow. Still, the dancers didn't seem to care and the chatter around the ballroom was now loud enough to be in contest with the band.

None of the Circle appeared to be dancing. The Wentforth sisters were seen to urge their partners on to the dance floor but this was firmly resisted by said partners. Wendy looked relieved; Isolde looked disgruntled. Gavin said apologetically that the last dancing he had done was Country Dancing in Skipton infant school and unless she wanted her toes treading on, would she mind excusing him? As the last dancing Annie had done was Grade three ballet at Dodo Milner's class, unless you counted the Time Warp at parties, which she very much didn't..., she was quite happy to excuse him. He was called over by a group of important-looking men and with a quick 'sorry' was gone. Annie wandered around the room.

There was hardly anything remaining of the hot buffet in the adjoining room at the other end of the ballroom. The waiting staff were clearing it away. It had looked delicious but she hadn't felt like eating much for some reason. What a night, she thought. Blizzard conditions, awkward company and not wanting to eat. It had hardly been worth coming and if Gavin didn't get together with Wendy after this, it would have been a total disaster. Although, thinking back with a warm glow to when Kit told her she looked beautiful, it might just have been worth it after all.

She looked across to see where Kit was and saw he was being talked at by Isolde. Isolde? What sort of a name is that? Ashton was now in deep and happy conversation with his tray-bearing friend. As she searched the room for Wendy, she ran up with Gavin. Annie noticed she was holding his hand tightly. Hurrah!

'I'm so sorry' he breathed as though he'd run a race, 'one of Alfred's mares is foaling and it may be a difficult birth, so we're going out to assist.' Gavin smiled at his willing assistant who smiled back.

'That's fine' replied Annie with more relief than was necessary. 'I thought Alfred kept pigs though, if it's the same Alfred you were talking to earlier. With the enormous shoulders like Al Capone and the skinny little legs.'

There was a pause before Wendy answered,

'Perhaps we should have explained, the horse belongs to my father, Alfred, who also keeps pigs.'

'Oh god, sorry.' Annie had the grace to blush but Wendy obviously wasn't going to let any slight to her father spoil the happiness of this chance with Gavin.

'It's alright' she smiled weakly, 'I've told him not to wear that suit.'

Gavin gave Annie a grateful smile before he turned round towards the door. As an afterthought, he shouted over his shoulder,

'If it takes too long, I'll give the keys to Doug, who we gave a lift to and he can take you all back down to the village. I might have to end up staying overnight here, sadly.'

Neither he nor Wendy looked the slightest bit sad. Annie saw their hands were still clasped tightly together and she smiled at them both.

'It's no problem at all so please don't worry. I might possibly, if I can get a lift down before, go a bit sooner, if that's alright?'

Of course he didn't mind she laughed to herself; he'd be deliriously happy but it gave him a get-out clause for his seemingly unchivalrous behaviour. He spluttered a thank-you and went off with Wendy in tow. In fact the evening had gone slowly downhill and she felt an urge to escape as soon as possible. She walked across to one of the floor-length windows and looked across what would have been a vast expanse of lawn but which now looked like the North Pole. It was still snowing but now in little slow-falling flakes instead of the earlier blizzard.

There were lights on the driveway and she could make out the tractor attempting another snow-clearing mission as some guests might want to leave earlier than they would normally.

Annie made a decision and found Doug and his wife to tell them she would be leaving early so not to look for her later. Then she went to the cloakroom and decked herself out in her Arctic explorer's outfit, taking a tip from Kit and wrapping the scarf over her mouth and nose. She made her way across the entrance towards the door. A lady who she had seen around the village, stopped her to talk about the weather and had she seen the frightful dress Avril Wentforth had on? After a couple of minutes, Annie made her escape, reflecting on the fact that, although the woman had been on the next table and ignored her, Annie had been more easily recognisable with ninety-five percent of her body covered up than she had been in an elegant evening gown. She would work out the psychological meaning of this later.

As Annie crunched into the snow at the bottom of the steps, she realised the hem of her dress would get soaking wet very quickly, so she hitched it up and tucked it into the top of her leggings, so she now looked like a very *plump* Arctic explorer. As she stood there with her coat pulled up and her thick black leggings on display, a deep voice behind her made her jump.

'I didn't realise they'd hired a stripper but wouldn't it be warmer inside?' Kit stood behind her, grinning as he looked her up and down. He was also ninety-five percent covered up, although maybe a little less as he'd left his mouth uncovered, all the better to laugh at her with.

'Are you going home too?' she asked, surprised. 'What about Isolde?'

'I told her when she asked me here that I would have to get back early as the dogs don't like being on their own at night for too long.'

They fell into step, cautiously making their way down the driveway with the light of the occasional reproduction street lamp showing them the way. Annie wouldn't admit it but she was grateful for the company. Especially *this* company. They walked on in silence for a little while, then…'Isolde asked you to the ball?'

'Yes' he sighed melodramatically as he started to explain, 'We've known each other since we went to the village school together. Not to sound arrogant, although it really does – she's always had a 'thing' about me. I've tried to keep it on a friendly basis and we have had other partners through the years but – she never seems to give up.'

Kit looked exasperated and then smiled to himself, shaking his head. 'She asked me to be her partner tonight because the man who was accompanying her originally had let her down because of the weather and she didn't want to lose face in front of everyone. I found out from Wendy after I arrived – because there's no love lost there – that it wasn't true. She knew she could rely on me not to let her down even though she must be aware of how I feel. There's just nothing there, do you know what I mean?'

'I do. Maybe you're going to have to be cruel to be kind and tell her the truth?'

'I have, so many times. If someone doesn't want to hear what you're saying, then they make their own excuses for why you're saying it.' He looked at her sideways. 'What about you with Gavin.'

'Oh no, there's nothing there at all' she exclaimed and then realised that it sounded uncaring. She explained about Wendy and why she'd agreed to go in the first place.

'So' she concluded, 'It seems we've all had our own agenda. I went because Gavin wanted to have a chance with Wendy, you went so Isolde wasn't partnerless and Ashton obviously went with Wendy to provide a substitute partner too, although he would obviously have rather partnered the wine waiter'

Kit laughed. 'Oh what a tangled web we weave…'

They had turned out of the driveway and towards the village. The only light was the white of the snow in the darkness but just then, the moon came out from behind a cloud and bathed the scene in ethereal moondust. The moonbeams caught the powdery flakes of snow as they fluttered down. Further ahead, the warm house lights at the village windows welcomed them as they slipped and slid towards them. Kit got hold of her arm and put it through his so they could anchor each other, or conversely, pull each other down if one of them fell!

Annie took in the view of the village below, surrounded by ghostly white hills in the distance with silver-covered trees lining their way forward. She felt very peaceful and content, despite the cold and the only sound was the scrunch of their boots, hitting the snow in unison. It was almost a spiritual experience, she thought. That is until she was interrupted by Kit.

'Pity you didn't bring your sledge with you.' He smiled innocently.

'It would have been no fun if I couldn't use you as a skittle though' she countered.

They walked on, arm in arm with conversation coming easily until they eventually reached Meadow Cottage. She reluctantly unlinked arms so she could get her key from the rucksack.

'Well, thank you for your company on the way back' she said awkwardly.

'It has been my pleasure' Kit replied, bowing low and kissing her hand. He turned to go and trying to prolong the moment she called after him,

'I hope the dogs are alright'

'Oh that was just my get-out clause when I became too bored. Goodnight Annie.' and he walked backwards, smiling that enigmatic smile that made her insides do the tango.

'Goodnight Kit' and she opened her door, trying very hard not to look back.

Chapter 14

Christmas Day morning arrived and Annie woke up feeling a strange mixture of elated – because of the magical walk home in the snow with Kit the previous night -and confused as she didn't know what her feelings were towards him or his towards her. She wasn't even sure she wanted to know the answer to either. She had come here to have a quiet life and to escape complications so she didn't want anything to change her peaceful life in Winterfell.

Gavin had sent her a text first thing to apologise, hoped she would have a good Christmas and could he pop in for five minutes tomorrow. She really didn't want any more apologies as she had been quite relieved when he'd defected over to Team Wendy but she knew he was due at his Aunt's at Mannington over twenty miles away for Boxing Day, weather permitting, so she didn't think he'd stay long.

The dale looked beautiful from her bedroom window. A white, unmarked expanse of snow covering every dale and fell; every tree and drystone wall. Thankfully there had been no snowfall since the night before but there was still no sign of activity outside. Everyone had their own preparations indoors, she supposed.

She had rung Lettie to wish her Merry Christmas and said that, yes, she would be with her on the thirtieth until the second of January if the trains were running and no, she wouldn't consider a sleigh pulled by Rudolph if they weren't.

She called for Maisie and they went together to Tom and Ada's to be met by Tom at the door with a Santa hat on and blowing a party trumpet that cut through the silence of the day and could probably be heard at the other end of the village.

'Come in, come in!' he said and everyone was so kind and welcoming that she even managed to get through the very sweet sherry she'd been handed. They exchanged presents and she received chocolates and a poinsettia. They all loved their Craft Centre presents, chiding her for spending 'too much' while visibly pleased.

All three of her neighbours chatted away, they'd known each other since schooldays but they always included Annie who was genuinely interested in their reminiscences, revelling in the stories of their younger days. These stories, said Tom, were all BHAS – before Health and Safety, as half their escapades would give today's nanny state an attack of the vapours.

She listened to the story of how Tom and Ada had finally got together after spending their school years mooning over each other with neither of them making a move. It was at a Christmas dance at the village hall, where everyone else had been doing the jive but neither of them had a clue. Annie suspected they were 'old-fashioned' even then, in a nice way. So Tom took her gently by the hand and led her outside where he waltzed with her on the small patch of frosty grass behind the hall, whilst humming Nat 'King' Cole's 'When I fall in love' in her ear.

Now, they were holding veined and wrinkled hands and gazing at each other as though they were still out there on that patch of grass, dancing in each other's arms. Annie's eyes were filling up and she looked across at Maisie who was wiping a tear away. Ada apologised for bringing old memories to the fore but wasn't that part of Christmas, thought Annie?

Maisie had a story of her own. She told Annie how she had met Theo in her forties as she had been married before to someone 'unsuitable'.

'And the least said about him, the better.' huffed Ada, outraged on her friend's behalf.

Maisie had dismissed the thought of ever marrying again, however Theo Brown had other ideas and she was very glad he had changed her mind.

He was a geography teacher at the nearest grammar school. Maisie was interested in local history and they had both volunteered on a dig nearby. Annie asked if Kit had known him with the archaeological connection. Maisie looked pleased and said that Theo was the reason Kit had taken an interest in archaeology in the first place. He had encouraged Kit when he was a young boy as Theo's own specialist degree included Geology, they could often be found with their heads together, analysing stones or recording them in a notebook.

'I only had my husband for nine years before I lost him to cancer' Maisie bowed her head as the tears sprang up again 'but they were the best years of my life and, even if it had only been one year, it would have been worth it.'

What lovely people, Annie thought, when suddenly Tom asked Ada if the turkey was alright and she shot out of her chair like a whippet at the race track. Luckily, the turkey was perfect and Annie enjoyed her dinner accompanied by, thankfully, happier anecdotes. They sat around the table for an hour or more, all wearing the party hats from their crackers. Annie's was bright orange and she was just glad that Lettie couldn't see her or the camera would be out. Tom managed to set a plastic spinning top off so it landed with a splash in his gravy. Ada tutted and told him to get on with it. Tom got his own back later as she put one of those red shiny paper fish from the cracker on her hand where it curled up tightly with the heat. Tom leaned across and said that meant she was hot and sexy while Ada's cheeks went as red as the fish.

Tom had a glass of beer to wash his dinner down and the ladies had lemonade but thought Annie might want something stronger, so Ada placed a can of shandy next to a tumbler, 'but we'll toast the Queen with another nice glass of sherry.' Annie couldn't wait...

They sat through the Queen's speech which was a first for Annie then she helped Tom wash the dishes up while the two old friends chatted away next door. After coffee, they played a raucous game of Land, Sea or Air where someone threw a cushion at you and you had ten seconds to think of inhabitants of the animal kingdom from the place that was shouted out. This resulted in Annie forgetting every fish she'd ever known when 'Sea' was shouted at her and also in Tom repeating 'Lion' three times for Land. 'You've got Lions on the brain lad' said Ada. 'You're not watching the Wizard of Oz later; it'll only make you worse.'

Afterwards Maisie said she would have to go home and sleep the huge meal off, if nobody minded. It seemed to bring the day to a natural conclusion and was Annie's cue to help Maisie on with her coat. They all said fond farewells to each other with plenty of hugs. The salt of the earth, every one of them, she thought. Everyone was pleased at how much Annie had enjoyed it and had fitted in and she truthfully told them that she fitted in better here than she ever had in her home town.

*

Sitting in front of the range in Meadow Cottage now with a bottle of wine, Annie felt quite depressed. It was almost a tradition with her, feeling sorry for herself at Christmas. Self-pitying ideas that only manifested themselves in the festive season. Maisie had told her that both Kit and Min preferred to spend Christmas Day by themselves, so she wondered if they had a bit of a 'feeling sorry for myself' day too. Although she could imagine that Kit had a 'what a waste of time Christmas is' day and Min probably had an 'I'm not going to lower myself to take part in provincial celebrations' day.

She actually liked spending Christmas by herself and got annoyed when people patronisingly felt sorry for her – but there was something about Christmas that brought up the image of families feasting and laughing together and pulled at the heartstrings. Annie remembered New Year's Eves that were bad too and was keeping her fingers crossed that this year would be different.

Even remembering the love and friendship between her neighbours and how quickly she had been accepted as one of them, choked her up. She didn't think she would ever find the kind of love they had all found.

And that set her off once more because, here she was 'Alone again, naturallee-ee' Tears poured down her face as the wine was poured into the glass. Stop the self-pity, she thought, you're pathetic Annie Millford. She went to switch the television on to cheer her up, something funny. It's a Wonderful Life' was just starting. She stared at it for a moment and then with a cross between a sniff and a sob, she turned it back off.

She didn't have enough tissues to get through that film.

Returning to the kitchen in a wave of nostalgia from next door, she got pie tins, pans and ingredients out and holding the memory of her lovely little gran's wonderful pastry, which made her sniffle again, she proceeded to make two huge meat and potato pies, a childhood favourite. By the size of them, they would last her until next Christmas. She would freeze one when they'd cooled and eat the other on Boxing Day for breakfast, lunch, dinner and supper.

While she was in a displacement activity kind of mood, she defrosted some raspberries and cobbled together a vague approximation of a trifle, which she would also pig out on tomorrow – and the next day – and...

She would put a stone on but no one would notice because no one cared, she thought, thoroughly enjoying her whinge-fest in a masochistic way. She sniffled 'Merry Blooming Christmas' to herself and raised her glass, which she found was mysteriously empty. As was the bottle.

The last thing she could fully remember doing was waltzing round the kitchen with an unopened bottle in one hand and a mince pie in the other whilst singing Slade's 'Well here we are, Merry

Christmas, everybody's having fun' at the top of her voice.

Chapter 15

Something woke Annie up from a night of strange dreams where she had been standing at one end of a valley and the Light Brigade had begun their charge. Seven hundred men on horseback galloping towards her with orange party hats on and with flashing fairy lights strung between them. All in all, she was glad she had woken up before she was either trampled or electrocuted.

She opened one eye tentatively. Eight-fifty a.m. the clock showed her accusingly. She slowly raised herself to a sitting position and stayed there until the room caught up with her. She went to the bathroom to clean her teeth when the cavalrymen started charging again, only this time she recognised it as the sound she had heard in her sleep – the sharp rat-a-tat of someone knocking urgently at her door.

'Grmmf' she grunted to herself and pulled on a thick fluffy dressing gown with pandas all over it, pulling it round her for warmth as she made her way down the stairs. Gavin stood on the doorstep looking very apologetic and very panicky.

'I'm really sorry' he stuttered 'I forgot you might be having a lay in but you said you'd always had sheepdogs?'

Annie blinked twice.

'I did, yes,' she said hesitantly, wondering what this had to do with the price of eggs – to quote her maiden Aunt.

'Well, Mr. Brindleton's sister Sally has had a fall and he's had to go to her. He may not be back for a day or two. I'm due at my Aunt's for lunch and overnight and I'm going to have to take it slowly as the minor roads aren't cleared yet and …'

He tailed off with a truly and pathetically apologetic look which Annie, in her current state, couldn't interpret. Until she followed where his eyes had come to rest and there, cowering behind Gavin's legs was a small sheepdog, looking timidly up at her with the most beautiful brown eyes.

'This is Chess' he announced as he attempted a hopeful smile. 'There's no one to look after her at the surgery now and she doesn't like being enclosed in a car. As you're used to this breed…'

Annie frowned and Gavin gulped.

'…I wondered if you wouldn't mind looking after her for a day or two, just till one of us is back?'

Annie stared at both of them, trying to weigh up which of them looked the most petrified – and took pity on them both. After all, she didn't have any plans for a few days.

'Yes of course I will' she replied as Gavin thankfully blew out all the breath he'd been subconsciously holding in. 'but I'm going away on the thirtieth so you'll have to be back before then.'

'We will, we will, you can't take more than a day or two off in this business and even then everyone complains. I've got all her stuff in the car, here – ' he said, handing her the lead while he went to fetch it. Annie and Chess looked at each other, both of them unsure but the dog's soulful eyes seemed to be full of hope. She shook her head to dispel that thought, she had always had an overactive imagination.

She pulled gently on the lead and Chess followed her inside. She took her straight into the kitchen where the low fire in the range was still churning out heat and sat in the chair to one side of it. Chess looked up at her unsure and Annie's heart melted. Smiling, she leant forward and stroked the black and white head for a minute and after a few seconds, the little dog seemed to relax and lay down at her feet. On her feet in fact, like a furry foot warmer.

Gavin came bustling in, dog bed in one hand and a huge laundry bag in the other which contained food, tablets, treats, toys and blankets.

'How long did you say you were away – two months?' she laughed.

'I'd rather bring too much than too little' he said, relaxing as he saw Chess. 'Well, she seems to have made herself at home. She's usually nervous around strangers but she seems to have taken to you very quickly.'

He looked pleased and bent down to stroke her.

'She was the runt of the litter and is still very small for her age. It was touch and go at first as to whether she would survive but she's got fighting spirit, although you wouldn't know it to look at her. She doesn't take much interest in anything and is frightened around other people and dogs, although she's not aggressive, she just seems to shrink into herself a little. Mr. Brindleton thinks she's depressed. Doggy depression. Which is quite possible, as implausible as it sounds. 'He stood up and handed her an A4 piece of paper.

'Amounts of food, when tablets are taken etc. She hasn't got a routine, she just lays there really

143

so don't worry if she won't go more than halfway down the lane on a walk, we have to practically drag her outside. And thank you, you've done us both a huge favour.'

'It's okay, nice to have a bit of company. How's Wendy?' she grinned as he opened the front door. His ruddy cheeks reddened even more.

'Yes, great' he grinned back, 'In fact I'm taking her out for a meal when I return.

Annie turned back to the kitchen as the door closed behind him. Chess had gone over to her bed at the other side of the Yorkshire range and now lay gazing up at her, searching this new human's face- and yes, Annie was sure now, it *was* hope she could see shining in those sad eyes.

Lithven Castle
N.W.Highlands
Scotland

Dearest Christopher

Happy Christmas!! We hope you received your present and card? We also hope you are having a nice time but I know you don't bother much with Christmas. I can't pretend we are happy at not having your company for the holidays, (Your grandfather is telling me not to make you feel guilty!) but we do understand and I know we will be seeing you soon anyway.

You mention the new resident, Annie, quite a lot in your letter... She seems very nice. Perhaps we will meet her next year? (My better half is saying 'Don't push it'!) I'm not at all – but I just hope you don't let your mother and father's relationship put you off, as you have in the past. Think of mine and Hugh's marriage – 63 wonderful years in September. You're welcome to come and wish us Happy Anniversary. In fact, you'd better!

Anyway, have a lovely Christmas, however you spend it. We'll be thinking of you.

All our love
G and G

Chapter 16

The next part of Annie's Boxing Day morning was spent having carbs in the form of a bacon sandwich, making herself look presentable and getting to know her small visitor.

Chess didn't seem to want to move from her bed although she would have to try and take her out to do the 'necessaries' before her neighbours got here. She had invited them for drinks, which would hopefully be tea or coffee considering what the smell of alcohol might do to her. She was just doing a few nibbles like crisps and nuts.

Annie had found them good company and hoped there would be more from their stock of stories. She was worried about Chess now though. Gavin had made it clear that she wasn't good with people but if she kept them in the sitting room it should be alright.

Right on cue, there was a knock at the door and Ada stepped in first while Tom helped Maisie in. They hugged her and started to go through to the kitchen.

'I've lit the woodburner in here for you' said Annie quickly, 'I thought these seats might be more comfortable for you.'

'Who's this then' asked Tom who was already through in the kitchen by then. 'Is this a Christmas present you haven't told us about?'

Annie had no doubt they'd have seen Chess being delivered by Gavin, alerted by the loud knocking. They missed nothing. Before Annie could say anything, he was bending down and stroking Chess who, although not looking overjoyed at the attention, was at least tolerating it. She warned the ladies that she might be a bit nervous so they both left it a couple of minutes before they went to fuss her. Chess accepted it with good grace then put her head back down on her paws.

'Tea, coffee or something stronger?' asked Annie and thankfully they opted for tea. She offered crisps, nuts and cheese straws before she remembered a packet of stem ginger cookies she'd picked up in the deli.

'Ooh, they sound nice' they chorused, so the plate went on the coffee table in the next room as they settled themselves on the settee and chairs near the woodburner. As she took the tea through, she saw Percy Brindleton, the vet, talking to someone by the church lych-gate over the road. He wasn't supposed to be here and she wondered if he knew that Chess was with her?

'Won't be a minute' she said and grabbing her coat, went across the road. Percy was talking to a small, pleasantly plump lady with a pudding basin haircut.

'Excuse me interrupting' Annie smiled at the lady 'but did you know that Chess is with me? Did Gavin tell you?'

'Yes, he phoned me. It was actually my idea in the first place. I couldn't get through to my sister's by car though. The pass is 'un-passable' he smiled. When I phoned to let her know, she told me she had refused to go to hospital anyway and the neighbour and her niece from the other side of town are helping out. It sounds more like bruises and shock from the fall, no bones broken, thank goodness. So I'm going up to see her by train, probably tomorrow if they're running okay because as Cynthia says, when you get as far as Denham, the snow is nowhere near as bad. Oh, sorry. Cynthia Blackwell, the new vicar. Cynthia, Annie Millford.'

'Hello' said Cynthia in a very friendly and enthusiastic way, holding her hand out.

Annie shook her hand and beamed back at her. What a difference from the last vicar.

'Well, shall I…?' said Percy, motioning towards Annie's cottage.

She nodded and didn't really know why she felt a reluctance to part with Chess, maybe because she looked so cosy in front of the range. Cynthia turned to go when Annie remembered her manners.

'Would you both like to come over for a drink, I have my neighbours in and I'm sure they'd like to meet the new vicar.'

'I'd love to' she laughed, 'I haven't met many people yet with the church unfortunately having to close up for this Christmas.'

They followed Percy across and he sat on one of the wooden chairs under the window, immediately chatting to Tom. Annie pointed Cynthia in the direction of the only other comfy chair in the room and left Percy to make the introductions. She noticed as Cynthia took off her coat that she had her dog collar on under a rainbow-coloured cardigan. She went to put the kettle on again and put out some nibbles.

'What would you like to drink?' she shouted through. Percy asked for coffee and Cynthia asked if she had any red wine otherwise any alcoholic drink would do. Annie went through and leant against the open door with a big smile on her face.

'You expected me to say tea, didn't you?' grinned Cynthia.

'I did and it just goes to show that I shouldn't stereotype. One red wine coming up.'

Over an hour later they were all still sitting there and the conversation showed no sign of drying up. There were the initial questions thrown at the vicar and an expression of regret at not having been able to sing the usual Christmas Eve carols in church. Then the conversation veered between being snowed in for days in nineteen-seventy-nine, Mrs Grantham's bad leg which didn't stop her going for a good gossip at the newsagents and a particularly salacious tale about Alfred Wentforth which Ada wouldn't let Tom finish, berating him for repeating unfounded gossip. Cynthia looked disappointed.

There was a lot of good-natured noise coming from the room and Annie kept tip-toeing through to check on Chess, who was sleeping through it all, not attempting to move. On her last check, Annie thought she really ought to take her up the lane, so she replenished the drinks and then clipped her lead on. Chess really didn't want to move but with a little vocal persuasion and a few gentle tugs on the lead, she eventually surrendered and reluctantly followed Annie to the front door. At the gate, Chess planted her feet and wouldn't move. Instead of turning right, down the hill, Annie tried turning left and Chess at least made a few steps in that direction although there was a lot of stopping and starting. As Annie crouched down in the snow, whispering encouragement, a voice close behind her made her jump.

'Hello Chess' it said and then Kit was by her side, stroking the dog's head. When he stopped, she nudged his arm for more. Annie was astounded and must have looked it because Kit started explaining.

'She can smell Bessie and Bella on me. Plus I've been to see her at quite a few times while she's been gaining her strength. I still feel guilty about it but I didn't even want to take on Bella until Percy persuaded me. He's got a devious way with him. They said they'd find another home for Chess but she's taking a long time to recover. Although they say there's nothing wrong with her physically…'

A puzzled frown appeared on his face and he stood up. They walked back down the lane and on impulse, Annie said,

'I appear to be having some sort of 'pop-up' Boxing day party, would you like to join us?'

Just then, a gale of laughter could be heard erupting from the cottage.

'What sort of parties do you hold Millford!' he laughed, 'I can't miss out on the fun. Thank you.'

'And the new vicar's here too. You'll want to meet the new vicar.'

'Will I?' he asked doubtfully.

'Definitely' replied Annie and they went inside.

*

Around 2 p.m., Annie's stomach rumbled loudly. She looked around her – no one had made a move and there was still much hilarity, especially as everyone now had a glass of wine in their hands. Even Ada and Maisie accepted a small glass of sherry from the bottle that Annie had bought specifically for her neighbours and Tom cradled a tot of whisky.

She suddenly thought of the two large meat and potato pies that were in her fridge. She hadn't got round to freezing the second pie, perhaps now she wouldn't have to. They couldn't go on forever drinking tea and wine and nobody seemed in a hurry to be off, even Kit. She felt quite awkward asking as she was aware she was an 'in-comer' to the village. Still, nothing ventured, nothing gained. She coughed.

'Erm, can I just say' they all looked in her direction, 'that in my fridge are two huge meat and potato pies I made last night. Would you do me an enormous favour and help me eat them today as otherwise I will inflate so much I won't be able to get out of the front door.'

The two older women looked at each other and then at Tom, who already had a 'Yes please' expression on his face. Percy immediately said,

'That sounds lovely if it's not too much trouble'

Ada said 'Meat and Potato pie, my grandma used to make that – my favourite.' Everyone said they'd love it and could they help - as they hadn't realised how hungry they were and then they fell to discussing what their grandmother's used to make.

Annie put the pies in the range oven and started to peel two bags of carrots and put some broccoli in a large pan. She had some peas in the freezer too and the gravy would come out of a supermarket tub. Gran wouldn't approve but she hoped her guests wouldn't mind.

Everything was nearly ready when Annie had a thought from nowhere. One Christmas-hater was here and apparently happy to celebrate Boxing day but the other Christmas-hater wasn't. She had a brainwave or so she hoped. She called Percy through.

'Would you mind very much going down for Minerva and asking her to join us for dinner' she asked.

'What a good idea, I was just thinking the same thing' he replied, adding that she might not want to come.

'Can you tell her she'd be doing me a favour or perhaps that she could meet Cynthia. Or...' Nothing seemed right.

'It's alright' said Percy, a look of understanding passing between them, 'I'll think of something.' And immediately she knew that Percy himself would be enough encouragement.

He passed Kit in the room where he was bending down to retrieve Maisie's handbag for her.

'Just off for Minerva.' he called on his way out.

'I can go for her if you want?' said Kit.

Annie stood back and caught Kit's eye, mouthing an exaggerated 'No-oo!' while shaking her head.

'No it's okay' Percy shouted back as he closed the door behind him and Kit started laughing.

'You little matchmaker! You're very observant and it would be nice to see them enjoying each other's company. They get on well on the rare occasions they can think of an excuse to see each other. I think Min invents illnesses for her cat and I think Percy is very aware of this but still goes. He doesn't charge her either.'

'Well it seems obvious to me' replied Annie with a grin. 'Just a minute, do you call her Min too?'

'It's a bit of a mouthful saying Minerva every time isn't it, although I wouldn't dare say it to her face.'

'My thoughts exactly. Where did you buy your handbag? I've been looking online for one like that.'

Kit looked down at the handbag he'd forgotten he was holding.

'Oh ha ha' he said at the moment Maisie asked if he could pass the bag as there were some photos she wanted to show the vicar.

Chapter 17

Min had come up for her dinner, although it was probably due to the presence of Percy more than anything else. Amazingly, during the course of the long meal, she had shed the bitter ice-maiden persona and became the warmer human being that had been lurking underneath. She joined in the laughter and even told a few funny stories of her own.

The pies, which had looked enormous when she took them out of the range oven, had disappeared, largely due to the extra-large helpings for the men. Tom was tutted at by Ada for cleaning out the last remains of the pie, straight from the tin with a spoon.

The trifle was almost eaten up too although everyone was full up and only wanted small portions. Unfortunately this led to an 'incident' where Annie tried to move the trifle bowl which had the remains of the jelly and custard sloshing about at the bottom. As she grabbed the bowl, Kit began to stand up to help but nudged the table as he did, throwing Annie off balance and sending the contents of the bowl all over his trousers.

It didn't help that Annie started to laugh. It didn't help that the others started laughing. It *did* help that Kit joined in the laughter as much as anyone and after cleaning the worst off with kitchen towel, asked to be directed to the bathroom.

Percy had told her that Chess wouldn't eat in company- or even if anyone was watching her- a throwback to not being able to get food from her mother because of her stronger siblings. Bearing this in mind, Annie suggested everyone went through and relaxed in the next room and she would bring coffee through there.

She managed to coax Chess over to a plastic mat near the back door where she ate a good portion of the food while Annie stood at the sink, pointedly ignoring her but glancing sideways all the time. She made a big fuss of Chess and said she was a good girl. Was it her imagination or did Chess look pleased? She walked her down the garden a short way. She seemed to prefer it when she wasn't on a lead. The fences looked secure and she didn't think she could get under the hedges. Annie hadn't really examined the garden yet because of the weather. Chess soon turned around and came back to the safety of her bed in front of the range.

From the sitting room came a chorus of 'Had an accident Kit?' and 'Didn't make it in time then?' followed by raucous laughter before the object of their ridicule made an appearance in the kitchen, where Annie doubled over at the sight of the huge wet patch over the front of his trousers where he had washed the remains of the trifle off.

'Minds in the gutter, all of you.' Kit said with a smile, raising his eyes to heaven.

He helped her make coffee and take it through while Min disappeared into the kitchen, taking her coffee. When she didn't reappear after five minutes and clattering noises reached her ears, Annie went through and saw her up to her elbows in soapy suds.

'I can do this later' said Annie 'go through and enjoy the conversation.'

'I'm not leaving all this to you, unless you have a dishwasher hidden away in these units somewhere?'

'No, no dishwasher, only me.' Annie grinned as she grabbed a tea towel.

'To tell you the truth,' Min continued 'It was a lovely thought to invite me to your delicious meal and the company has been wonderful – but I'm so used to being on my own that it is a bit overwhelming, so I'm escaping for a few minutes.'

'Yes, you get used to the peace and quiet don't you?'

'Did you live on your own before here then?' said Min frowning, as though it hadn't occurred to her.

'Yes, for many years. Work took over really and a few bad choices in men put me off, possibly forever' she laughed and then gave her a brief resume of her life as they washed up at the sink overlooking the snow-filled garden.

In the same spirit, Min came out with the revelation that she had been brought up by her terminally hippie parents in a kibbutz in Israel, a commune in Morocco and finally, a spiritual retreat in Devon which came very close to being a cult. She escaped from it when she was sixteen and for two years, came to live with her grandmother in this very village. In fact in the very cottage that Min herself lived in now. It had been rented by her grandmother but as soon as she had seen it for sale five years ago, she bought it. It held probably the only good memories she had of her younger days. When her grandmother sadly died she took herself off to a theological college, training to be a priest as she was searching for the spiritual side she had been brought up to believe in but after nearly two years, decided it wasn't for her.

This was a complete surprise to Annie who, as she thought Min was a witch, did not see that coming.

'You look shocked.' Min said quietly.

There was an elephant in the room and it wasn't budging. Annie thought it was time she started pushing it out.

'Min? Erva…!' she spluttered.

'It's alright, you don't have to keep adding the last bit on, I don't mind Min.'

'Really? Thank goodness, it's a bit of a mouthful.'

'Named after the Goddess Minerva. Percy and I discovered some common ground walking up here. He was named after a demi-God, the son of Zeus.'

'Percy the demi-God?' asked Annie, puzzled.

'He was christened Perseus - but for heaven's sake don't mention it to anyone' she implored as a grin appeared on Annie's face.

'I wouldn't dare' she laughed and then remembered what she was going to ask in the first place.

'Min. About the Winter Solstice…'

'I'm a Druid' said Min, calmly.

'A Druid! Ah, I thought you were a witch' she blurted out before she could stop herself.

'No, not a witch' laughed Min, turning round as the others started filing through with their cups. She leaned down and whispered in Annie's ear. 'That's Marje.'

Annie stood with her mouth open. Well, she thought, this was anything but the peaceful, ordinary, nothing-ever-happens little village she thought it was. Boring was not a word you could apply to Winterfell.

Ada dragged Tom off home after saying how much they'd enjoyed themselves but Tom was nodding off – 'no wonder with the amount of food he put away' she tutted – and his snores were drowning out the conversation. They hugged Annie and thanked her profusely.

The vicar departed reluctantly but not before saying what a lovely community she had moved to and how much she was looking forward to her tenure here now.

Kit put the kettle on, washed up the cups and asked if anyone wanted another coffee as he was getting one. Annie watched him make himself at home and decided she liked it. He turned and she smiled at him in a hazy way as he fixed her with those lucent brown eyes which normally seemed to be smiling at a private joke but now seemed more intense. How long they stood like this she wasn't sure but it felt like time stood still.

'Are you having coffee?' said Percy in her ear and the moment was gone.

As they all finished off the day in front of the woodburner in the sitting room, conversation dwindled to a pleasant hum as the food, drink and heat caught up with them. Annie started to feel pleasantly tired and relaxed.

As she dangled her arm over the chair side, her hand met with a furry head, followed by a weight leaning against her legs. Chess looked up at her trustingly as Annie stroked her head, hardly daring to breathe as she didn't want her to go slinking back to her bed in the kitchen. Chess lay down, apparently happy to be by her side. Nobody noticed this momentous occasion apart from Kit, who was looking across at her and smiling, giving her the faintest of nods. Did Percy glance across too, although he'd turned back when she tried to catch his eye.

Maisie yawned and said she was dropping off so she'd better get home. Kit said he'd see her in safely before he went home to the dogs. Min said it was the best Boxing day she had ever had and Percy, after planting a chaste thank you kiss on Annie's cheek, said he'd see Min back if she was ready. Min stood next to him eagerly. Of course she was ready smiled Annie to herself, she'd been ready for years and perhaps Percy was now feeling the same way?

Percy looked at Annie.

'I'll get the lead then shall I? Take her back?'

Everyone turned to look at her and Chess, aware of an undercurrent, sat up again, this time planting her head firmly on Annie's lap and fixing her with those soulful eyes.

'No, you can leave her' replied Annie, 'In fact, if it's alright you can leave her here permanently? I think Chess has found her new home.'

Maisie clapped her hands together in glee and came over to hug her while Kit whispered,

'Good call Annie and thanks for everything today.'

Percy, who Annie suspected had set her up for this from the start, nodded and looked as pleased as punch. As did Min but for a different reason.

As they thanked her and went on their way, Annie and Chess sat there for the rest of the evening, warm and relaxed and just happy in each other's company.

DIARY

A valuable lesson learned. I must learn not to judge so harshly on first appearances. In fact, I think there is a valuable lesson there for us all, including Annie as her first impression of Kit was that he was a Tramp! Although it has to be said that he has eclectic taste when it comes to clothes and my first impression was that he was from the Victorian age!

Back to Annie. She couldn't be more different to how I'd imagined her - as a lady of leisure without a care in the world. Apparently, she worked herself into the ground before she took this sanity-saving break. She is very kind and has just adopted a sheepdog. She still appears to be scatter-brained though, despite her obvious intelligence. Witness the trifle-throwing over Kit's trousers which I have to admit was quite funny.

She is also most definitely intuitive. Although she doesn't say anything, I think she realises that I rather like Percy Brindleton and appears to be trying to throw us together. This may be a little ambitious of her as I have been trying to do the same thing for years but I have come to the conclusion that he only sees me as an acquaintance from the village.

It's nice to be thrown in his company more often though as Annie is nothing if not sociable. She seems to cram everyone in that small cottage she is renting. She even managed to invite the new vicar, although she'd never seen her before. The vicar is a cheerful and fairly loud person, full of bonhomie. Vast improvement on the Reverend Wellingport.

I know that the Reverend and Farmer Gardman had seen me up at the Stone more than once. Luckily I'd seen them before they saw me and was halfway down the path. They tended to shout things like 'The Devil is upon you!' and 'You will be damned forever and go straight to Hell.' I just shout back a Druidic blessing at them like 'May the Blessed sunlight shine on you.' to show that I can rise above their invective. Although sometimes it hurts. There should be room for all beliefs in the world without half of them condemning the other half.

Back to Annie again. She can't help herself interfering though. We were saying how nice the new vicar was and she said she thought my hair would look nice done like hers! I said 'but it looks like a pudding basin!' and she said 'not quite like that but a little longer, in a short bob. I think it would really suit you. And a little lighter maybe?'

Did she really think I was born yesterday? I know my hair is so short it looks like a shaving brush but what does it matter as nobody pays me any attention anyway? Well yes, I didn't tell her but I dye my hair black. In a way, it might be easier to go back to my nondescript brown. Although it would probably be grey by now, judging by the regrowth on my parting. A horrible thought. Am I ready for that? My hair though is my own business, as is the rest of my appearance, thank you very much!

Strange though. Annie very kindly gave me a Christmas present. I hadn't got one for her so I went down to the stationer's this morning and got her one of those leather-backed pocket-size sketch pads, which she seemed really pleased about when I dropped it off. She even gave me a hug. Her present to me though was a stained-glass sun-catcher for the window - and there, staring back at me were not only Leofric, my black cat but both the other cats I have had in my life.

Ptolomy the marmalade cat and Cleo the tabby. How did she know? She really must be intuitive.

I had to smile at Annie's surprise at me being a Druid. It was less that I was a Druid and more because I wasn't a witch, as she'd thought. I didn't get the chance to ask if she knew anything about Druidism. Perhaps that's a conversation we can have in the future. Maybe I'll invite her down here for coffee.

I wonder if Maisie mentioned to her that her husband Theo had written a book on Standing Stones and Druidic Imagery? He was very interested in Druids and had talked to my grandmother extensively, quoting her in the book. I have a copy and so does Kit.

I will perhaps tell Annie, at some point, that my grandmother was a Druid. And that it's the reason I became one. Because my grandmother was the Guardian of the Stone as her father had been before her and for generations before that , going back into the mists of time. This is why I have always felt I belonged here, the only place I have ever called home. It skipped a generation with my mother but the universe has aligned again and I have taken over the mantle . I am the Guardian of the Winterfell Stone.

Grant, O Great Spirit, Thy
Protection;
And in protection, strength;
And in strength, understanding;
And in understanding, knowledge;
And in knowledge, the knowledge
of justice;
And in the knowledge of justice,
the love of it;
And in that love, the love of all
existences;
And in the love of all
existences, the love of the Earth
our mother, and all goodness.

Druid's Prayer (Iolo Morganwg)

Eostre

(The beginning of Spring, named after the
Goddess of rebirth and of the radiant dawn)

Chapter 18

Annie rushed round putting all the chairs out in the library meeting room, ready for the talk tonight. Since the 'entente cordiale' between her and Min, she had offered to help her in the library and now worked there on Wednesday mornings. This meant that Min could have the whole of Wednesday off as it was only open till one p.m. because of market day.

She also worked alongside Min every other Saturday morning as it was a busy time. She didn't like to commit to any more time there as she didn't like to leave Chess more than a few hours. Min had said she could bring Chess with her but the little dog hadn't settled and preferred sleeping and waiting in front of the range at home.

There was a bad moment when Annie realised her ticket was booked for Scotland and she had promised her friend this New Year visit. She had asked Gavin to look after her for two more nights while she went but Chess realised something was wrong as soon as Gavin put her on a lead, especially when he turned right through the gate and not on her usual walk. She dug her heels in and refused to go any further, probably thinking she was being taken away from Annie and back to the vets permanently. Gavin came up trumps though and looked after her in Annie's house, sleeping in the spare bedroom. During the day, Maisie came in and dog-sat and formed a bond with her canine companion. Chess made a fuss of Maisie every time she saw her now but stuck her nose in the air and refused to acknowledge the existence of poor old Gavin.

The New Year at Lettie's was predictably chaotic but it was so good to see everyone especially their gorgeous little boy Hamish who called her Anyan as that was the nearest he could get to Auntie Annie.

When she got back home, as she now thought of Meadow Cottage, Annie spent quite a few hours drawing appealing sketches of Chess, which she showed to Lettie on their next Zoom meeting – and so 'Chessie the Rescue Dog' idea was born. She had been working on that now, from Lettie's storyline, for a couple of months and the preliminary sketches had already been sent up to the publishers for approval.

Annie had started taking Chess for regular walks past Kit's house and up to the Stone regularly and from the start Bessie recognised her other daughter. Bella would have been enthusiastic over any dog so it was hard to know if she recognised Chess as her sister but gradually, with Kit joining her regularly on walks, the three dogs had become good friends. Percy had said he scarcely recognised the scared little dog that had left their house. She would never be anything other than quiet, it was her nature but now she looked happy, had energy to spare and her coat shone.

On one of these occasions in mid-January, Kit said he had something for Annie so she followed him into his house after their walk. She caught a tantalising glimpse of his study again but got no further as he brought out a parcel wrapped in sturdy brown paper, with 'Annie' written on the front. It was a copy of his latest book about the late Neolithic people.

He explained that there were many references to Megaliths and Stone Circles so he thought she might be interested. She thanked him and told him she had been going to buy one when it was on general sale and he seemed pleased. She too was pleased as she caught sight of the Acorn paperweight actually doing the job she bought it for. His desk did look tidier but it could be because he had finished writing the book now.

She brought herself back to the present. It was Kit who was giving the talk tonight, wanting to explain to anyone who was interested from the village and beyond, about the importance of the Winterfell Stone to the community and its historical significance. He had been away at a dig for nearly all of February up in the Highlands and took the dogs, so he must have been renting a cottage somewhere near. He hadn't been back long. Annie finished putting out the chairs and made sure the information flyers were on the side tables. Kit would set the PowerPoint up later.

As she wandered back through to the main library, she smiled to herself as she caught sight of Min. She had completely transformed herself. Her hairdresser had dyed her hair to match the regrowth from the black and it was a fetching shade of silver-grey. It now reached just above her chin in a flattering bob. Instead of her stuffy, formal suits which made her look as though she was going into the law courts, her clothes were now softer and more feminine.

Today, she had on a blue round-necked jumper with a darker blue and white floral print skirt which came down to mid-calf. Annie recognised it as the one in the charity shop she had pointed out for her to try on, only to be met with a glare from Min. She *had* tried it on though and it really did suit her.

Looking at her now, Annie realised she'd lost weight too. She had heard many people at the library compliment her on her appearance. Surely Percy can't have failed to notice the new Minerva Jones. Although as she recalled his usual 'on a different plane of existence' expression where his eyes glazed over, lost in thought, she could easily believe it had passed him by.

Now to pop down to the village for milk for the countless cups of tea she hoped she would be handing out at the meeting. She hoped for Kit's sake – and for the village's version of a pressure group, the Stone Circle- that it was well attended.

Standing stone, information.. Please take one.

MENHIR (Standing Stone). A tall, unworked, large-sized stone block usually placed vertically, often reached large sizes of 20 feet or more. A circle of vertically arranged large stones, which form a more complex megalithic group are often built around a menhir.

Areas on which megalithic monuments are located create a uniquely mysterious aura; they intrigue, stimulate the imagination, and often evoke the feeling of communing with something supernatural. Since the dawn of time, these places have been surrounded by a specific cult, playing an important role in the development of civilization.

Megaliths are the basis of many legends which for centuries have been etched into the subconscious of ordinary people and of entire nations. They have always been important to communities as a focus for their spiritual existence.

Chapter 19

Kit entered the meeting room, his coat flying out behind him. His rain-drenched unruly curls and his long strides giving the impression of Darcy striding from the lake in TVs Pride and Prejudice. Annie had given him so many personas since she arrived that it was no wonder that she couldn't quite get to the real Christopher Courtney behind them.

His expression didn't tempt Annie to ask what was wrong because if he'd turned to look at her, he could have lasered her to death with his eyes. He put his laptop down on the table at the front, stayed in that position for at least ten seconds and then, taking a deep breath, he slowly turned around. Annie didn't know whether to run, duck or offer a quivering sympathetic smile. She decided on the last which, luckily, was returned.

'Sorry, I didn't see you there' explained Kit. 'I've just had a conversation with Gardman. I've offered to buy the land from him. The greedy always love money and a damn good deal but unfortunately, he loves spite and self-righteousness more. He refused point blank.'

He walked towards her with a grim expression on his face.

'Don't worry, I'll have calmed down by the time everyone arrives. Has there been much interest?'

'Apart from the usual suspects of our Stone Circle group, we're not sure. Min says there have been quite a few asking about the notice on the door.'

'We'll just have to wait and see then. I'm grateful for any local support in this, on an emotional level rather than a practical one.'

Kit still didn't look too happy. Min poked her head around the door.

'Maisie, Ada and Tom are here a bit early, is it alright to let them in?'

'Of course' smiled Kit, at least pretending to brighten up as he grabbed Maisie's arm to guide her. His fondness for her was obvious. He showed them to the front seats.

'Pride of place for diehard supporters' he said.

Others from the 'Stone Circle' started to drift in and other people joined the meeting either from solidarity or curiosity. While not overflowing, the room was soon gratifyingly full.

Min began the meeting by welcoming Kit and introducing him to those who didn't know him as there were quite a few non locals there. Annie noticed that Percy had put his jacket on a seat next to him but while Min was talking, someone had slipped into the seat. Mrs. Whitehouse, who was also sweet on Percy as she was always calling him to come and check on her Irish wolfhounds for non-existent ailments according to Gavin. Annie couldn't see Percy's magnetic attraction herself but he was a lovely bloke all the same. He certainly didn't look pleased now at having to move his jacket for his stalker.

Gavin was also there with the love of his life Wendy who was actually rather a sweet girl. Her sister Isolde had also plonked herself at the front and was now making cow-eyes at Kit even though she was practically engaged to Sir Anthony Graveley. Some people were just greedy, thought Annie.

As Min walked past Mrs Whitehouse, she gave her a look that would have frozen fire then came to sit with Annie at the back. Annie smiled to herself but then realised she had been thinking uncharitable thoughts about Isolde too, so perhaps her and Min weren't that different. She sat up with a start. Why should she be thinking about Kit like that? Kit had never given any indication that they were anything other than friends. Apart from a couple of smouldering looks which penetrated her heart and committed them to eternal memory. Could she have been mistaken in the intensity of those looks? He certainly hadn't given her any encouragement since but at least seemed to enjoy her company on dog-walks.

Kit's voice brought her round.

'So here we have some Megaliths. I will be showing you sarsens, cromlechs, menhirs and burial mounds so that I can explain the significance of our own Winterfell Stone and any possible stone circle surrounding it.'

He flashed views of various places up on the large screen, including the whole of the British Isles, India, France and Bulgaria – explaining their significance as he went on.

'As you can see, some, like the well-known Menhir at Rudston in Yorkshire, more commonly known as Rudston Monolith, are stand-alone stones and no trace of a circle around them has been found apart from one small stone nearby at Rudston.

This may possibly be the case with the Winterfell Stone but we would at least like the chance to find out. There is evidence in early books that there were other stones there but they were deemed too insignificant to be of any importance. I beg to differ. If there is a stone circle or part of a stone circle around our stone, then we can ascertain the original purpose.

If this proves to be the case, we in the Prehistory Society believe that rather than a random stone which may have been deposited there in the ice age according to some theories, it could have been a gathering place for the Neolithic community around this area.

As well as using it as a market place, they could have had ceremonial gatherings there. Giving thanks to the sun for continuing to bless their land with warmth and light. The sun was incredibly important to these superstitious people as without it, they couldn't produce their crops, feed themselves and keep alive. They probably thought the sun itself was a god.'

'Were there any sacrifices there?' shouted a voice.

'Adrian' whispered Min in her ear and did an eye roll. Ah, Adrian the *proper* taxi driver, thought Annie.

'Unlikely' answered Kit 'but we can't rule it out. Earlier peoples may have sacrificed humans but later on, at the probable time of our Stone, it would have been mostly animals if there were to be sacrifices. Why Adrian, were you thinking of anyone in particular?' Kit threw back at him.

'Aye, the wife for a start!' Adrian replied to a chorus of chuckles while the skinny little woman at his side dug him in the ribs.

'Or perhaps your husband, Mrs M.? It can be arranged?'

'There'll be more flesh to sacrifice with him, at any rate' she grinned, patting his ample stomach.

The laughter died down after a while and then Kit explained about the probable ceremony and its significance. About the Priest or Elder of a community leading a procession up to the ancient stones with other people following in order of importance.

'I don't want to upset any Christians here tonight because as I said, there is a place for us all in this world. Yet remember how we were taught at the time in schools that these people were backward in their worship of the elements. How we all laughed when he saw pictures in our books of these people bending down to worship the sun. I firmly believe that everyone should have their own faith and that every faith has its own importance to the people who follow it and to the world as a whole – from the Greeks and the Romans to the Christian faith of today. Yet can we deny that Neolithic people were right? Rather than worship something they couldn't see or feel – or even imagine- they chose to worship something they could see above them in the sky, that gave them warmth and light, that made their food grow.

To me, that isn't primitive, it's just common sense. Like worshipping the full moon for lighting the darkest of nights, the earth beneath their feet that nourished the crops they planted and water for helping things to grow lush and green.

Remember, these people had no idea of what the cosmos was. They had no means of knowing if this wonderful yellow orb in the sky wouldn't just disappear. So they kept on the right side of this life-giving deity by worshipping it at least once a year. The most important time being the Summer solstice or an approximation of it. They would know from years of observation when the longest day should be due and the ancient stone above our village would have made this more accurate with the position of the sun according to the stone. This theory is yet to be proved but it is known that they gathered at these monuments around the summer solstice, so to me, it lends the theory much credibility. This is almost scientific stuff when you think about it.

This is why I believe that the Winterfell Stone should be investigated, for evidence that it was a gathering place for the community, like a prehistoric village square. I am not denying that any findings on this site would be significant for the Prehistory Society but I'm interested more on a local level. This is my village and it is our ancestors who may have done all the things I've described. This ancient site may have been important to our communities for thousands of years. It is our history and our heritage and it needs to be reclaimed.'

A few cheers rang out and people applauded. Kit looked embarrassed at his impassioned speech so Min stood up.

'Have you heard anything from Mister Gardman yet?' She spat out the word 'mister' as though it was a nasty taste in her mouth.

'Unfortunately yes' replied Kit, the angry look back on his face. 'As some of you know, I've offered to buy the land from Gardman at above the going rate. He turned it down flat. There was no reason to turn down a very good offer for pasture on the perimeter of his land which he only cuts once a year for hay and rarely uses for grazing. Most of us know it's for no other reason than he, along with our erstwhile vicar, thinks we're all pagan devil-worshippers and that we are going to use it to prance around naked, have orgies and pledge allegiance to Beelzebub.'

'Apart from Beelzebub, it sounds alright to me' came the earlier voice belonging to Adrian.

'If tha' pranced about naked lad' came his wife's voice 'that'd scare everyone else away!'

Laughter erupted again, eliminating the serious tone the meeting had taken. Kit laughed and shook his head.

'To continue, he said, 'Alfred Wentforth very kindly gave us permission to dig on his land but it only goes as far as the ancient woodland according to the ordnance survey map, and the woodland is protected anyway, so sadly his offer can't be taken up. Gardman's field abuts my land but as the Stone is almost half a mile from my boundary, there's no point digging there either. We've applied, of course, to list it as a protected ancient monument but they can't compulsory purchase it unless the owner tries to develop the land to the detriment of the monument, which he hasn't. Although I dread to think of the damage his tractor is doing in his yearly haymaking to any potential stones underneath those 'bumps' in the field.

We're at a stalemate and need Gardman to be on our side. All we are asking is permission to dig and occasional access to the Stone afterwards.

Another voice rang out

'Is it possible that he, as well as others amongst us, are worried about the village becoming a tourist hotspot with all sorts of weirdos coming to see it.

There was a murmur of dissent around the room at this observation but Annie could understand his point of view. She wondered how Kit would answer it.

'I can assure you on Gardman's behalf that while it may be one of his reasons, there is a remarkable degree of cussedness to his refusal. He also knows exactly what I'm going to tell you now as it was part of our 'discussion'.

'There are only two entrances to the site. One is the footpath on Alfred Wentforth's land which as most of you know, is private but he kindly allows the villagers to use it to walk their dogs. The part before you reach the wood is overgrown so the stone can't be reached only across private land from the Hall. The other is down a private road alongside my property.

If I had managed to buy the land, these entrances would have remained private to the general public. Maybe a few times a year the site could open for the day with access from mine or Mr.Wentforth's land, perhaps for a fete to celebrate Spring or Summer. Or perhaps a folk festival, something that could raise money for the village and other local causes. Nothing that would damage the Stone or any other stones we might find, these would be jealously guarded, but just the area around it so people could see the monument.

Villagers and locals would be able to see it whenever they wanted as usual, as long as they phoned us first to okay it with us. If I had managed to buy it, it would still have been private land but I had hopes of the whole village celebrating the Summer Solstice there – and the Winter one for the hardier souls. Perhaps May Day too as I know the village follows this old tradition.

But no, absolutely no access for the general public. The Winterfell Stone belongs above all, to the village of Winterfell and its people, so I can put your mind at rest on that point Mr Brame.'

Mr Brame nodded, apparently satisfied, as did others who had obviously worried about the same thing. Well done Kit, thought Annie.

'So, to conclude, we need your support. Minerva and Annie have printed flyers, one explaining a little about standing stones and the other asking for suggestions of how you can support us. Keep it clean please and that means you…' he pointed. Everyone laughed and turned to Adrian who held his hands up in mock innocence. He was obviously well known as the village joker.

Soon all the tea was drunk, the biscuits were eaten and almost all of the flyers were gone. Annie had noticed that Percy walked away as he was being talked at by an overbearing Mrs Whitehouse and came to talk to Min.

'Can't stand that woman' Annie heard him whisper to Min, who looked like the cat who'd got the cream.

Kit came striding down to the back of the hall. 'All the flyers gone? Good. Do you think it went alright then? I didn't come across as too aggressive did I?' Annie's heart went out to him, he looked genuinely concerned.

'I think you struck just the right balance, passionate about the Stone and its history but predominately you came across as caring about your village. I really enjoyed it and learnt a lot.'

Kit unexpectedly put his arm around her and squeezed her to him.

'That's my girl- and thanks for your help.'

She couldn't help but notice Isolde's sour expression as she chose this moment to walk past them and out of the door. Annie had a feeling that Min might have to share that saucer of cream with her as she tried to stop a silly grin spreading over her face.

DIARY

That Mrs Stuck up Hyacinth - Bucket-Whitehouse! With her French-pleated hair and her perfume that hangs round her like a foul, pungent smog. Making a play for Percy that was so obvious that she might as well have worn a notice pinned to her matronly, sagging chest saying 'Take me Percy, I'm yours!'

I must say though that I was very pleased when Percy came to me straight away afterwards. Apparently she makes it obvious he is the object of her affection when he is called out to her dogs. He's started sending Gavin now, where at all possible.

Unfortunately, I think he still just sees me as a friend, which of course is all I want to be I suppose. It was nice though to hear him say 'What have you done to yourself lately Minerva? I can't put my finger on it but you seem softer and more smiley'. He means well and I'm very glad the new hairstyle and clothes are working. I mean, not that it matters - I didn't do it just for him of course. When I dissected his statement later, I thought it probably meant that he thought I was a hard, miserable bitch before! So thank you Annie. You're wise beyond your years and not once have you said 'I told you so'.

Speaking of Annie, I saw her throwing visual daggers at Isolde yet that relationship never got off the starting blocks. When Kit gave Annie a hug after the meeting, she looked very happy.   So did Kit. I wonder…?

Chapter 20

The sun shone through the windows, inviting Annie to get out and feel its warming rays. Spring was present in the atmosphere even though it wasn't quite official yet. Going through to the kitchen she saw that Chess had finished her breakfast and was standing at the back door with an eager expression.

'Okay, quick walk down the garden and then we'll go and see your family, if that's alright with you madam?'

Chess replied with the trademark panting smile of the sheepdog and seemed very happy with the arrangements. Annie had ventured down the garden every day when the snow had finally gone. It was a long thin garden, separated from Maisie by a long, shoulder-high hedge. Annie's shoulder that is, as Maisie completely disappeared behind on her side. There was a five-foot gap immediately at the back of their houses and her and Maisie had placed a chair outside each of their cottages and chatted away with a cup of tea in their hands on the few warm days they'd had so far.

The hedge on Tom and Ada's side was even higher but she could sometimes see Tom's pork pie hat travelling, seemingly of its own volition, along the top of the hedge at his side. Further down towards the bottom, the hedges had been trimmed right down to take full advantage of the sun. This was the last place the sun stayed in their gardens and each cottage had a hardstanding area there, where they could set up a table and chairs and enjoy the last warming rays. They could watch as the sun started to set behind the distant hills that bordered the dales and fields. There was an unused path running along the bottom that ran up to Kit's private lane. It was very overgrown and now served as a thin strip of wildlife meadow instead.

As Annie reached the end of her garden and went to perch on a rickety old bench, she heard a 'BOO!' and nearly fell off it. Tom popped his head up and started laughing at her expression.

'Sorry, did I make you jump? Now then old lass' The last part being meant not for her but for Chess who had jumped up to the hedge to be made a fuss of. 'Grass'll be growing soon. I can come round with my mower if you like?

Annie looked at the large strip of grass running the length of the garden with a path to the far side.

'You've got enough to do Tom, with all those vegetable beds of yours. There's a hover mower in the shed, I'll get it out soon and have a go.

'Aye well, easily maintained your garden anyway' he said with a disapproving note. Instead of 'easily maintained', Annie heard Tom's 'bland' replacing it.

'It could definitely do with some brightening up. I'm going to put some pots up at the top for ease of watering but I wondered if I'd be able to dig a flowerbed by the side of the path. It would bring colour all the way down. Or perhaps in that box thing over there' she said, pointing across the patio.

'That's a box for planting veg in is that. Raised off t'ground on legs, supposedly away from slugs and snails. You could grow a fair few things in there. If you wanted, I could start you off – tell you what to plant and when? I've got some seedlings coming on, I could let you have some of those.'

Tom was never happier than when he was discussing gardens.

'I'd really like that Tom' replied Annie.' I'm not sure about the flower beds though. I can ask them at the letting agents?'

'Yes, I think the Prestons wanted it an easy maintenance garden as they weren't up here every week-and even less recently- and didn't want to spend all their free time gardening. Veg'll be alright though in that box. And we can start you off with some potatoes you can grow in sacks.'

'I think I'll do that Tom, thanks. I'll start looking for some pots to plant up too, I think I saw some in the hardware shop.'

Chess came up to stare at her with her head cocked to one side, ears pricked up and tongue lolling in an open mouth.

'She allus looks like she's laughing when she does that' Tom smiled.

'What she's actually doing' said Annie 'is asking me why we're hanging about here when there's walks to go on and dogs to meet.'

Five minutes later they were out of the front door and off up the lane.

*

Bessie and Bella raced down Kit's garden to greet Chess and Annie, barking at first then whining as they knew this meant a walk. She looked up and saw Kit outside his front door, mobile clutched to his ear, while pacing up and down. There followed an example of long-distance sign language where Kit pointed at the phone and shook his head. Then Annie pointed at the dogs and then up the lane towards the Stone. Then Kit nodded exaggeratedly, while she let the dogs through the gate. Then Kit shrugged his shoulders with an apologetic look on his face. Annie did the thumbs-up sign, which he returned. Off she went, contemplating the idea of starting their own Mime Theatre.

All three dogs behaved perfectly off the lead on this well-known walk at least. They ran off down the lane at fifty miles an hour to work off their energy but then came trotting back to her, pretend-fighting on the way. They obviously wished that people had four legs too and could move a little quicker than this snail's pace, then they wouldn't have to keep coming back to check on their humans. They repeated this ad nauseam, all the way to the Stone, therefore getting twice the exercise.

They stood at the edge of the wood. The dogs had been told many times not to go any further and being a particularly intelligent breed, they knew they had to stick to it. The Winterfell Stone seemed to fascinate them as much as it did humans and Annie had to smile as she looked down at them to see all three, in a row, facing towards the Stone.

It was mesmerising though. There was something in the stone, minute blue particles that caught the light occasionally, making it more impressive than usual. These particles were glinting in the sun now and Annie wished more than ever that she could just go over and touch it. Just lay her hand flat against the Stone and feel the spirit of centuries past, course through her veins. There was something primeval about the hypnotic pull these great stones had on the human psyche – as though it was in the blood of the human race but they had long ago forgotten why.

By the time they had walked back, there was still no sign of Kit. She let the dogs into the garden and not wanting to just walk off without a word, she went up and knocked on the door. Hearing a voice, she opened it slightly until the dogs barged past her and ran up the passageway.

'Kit?' she shouted.

'In here, come through' and she went in the direction the dogs had taken. He was sitting in a large high-backed chair at the end of an old farmhouse table. He had his head back and his eyes closed.

'Hi' he said quietly.

'You okay?' It was obvious he wasn't.

'I've just used my last option up for the Stone. That's it. The combined might of every archaeological and historical society, the government, local councils, God and everyone else you can think of, has failed. *I've* failed. There's nothing else I can do. I might as well give up.'

'No Kit…' she protested. She had never seen him like this. He was almost always cheerful when this subject wasn't brought up and when it was he was annoyed, angry but never despondent.

'After all, what is it for?' he continued. '*Who* is it for? Am I doing it for selfish reasons to prove something to myself? Am I doing it out of a misguided sense of loyalty to a culture I respect and a village I love? Do they really want to discover more about the Winterfell Stone or am I just deluding myself and they're just going along with me to appease my obsession? I really don't know if it is worth fighting any more. So many years now and I'm no further than I was at the start.' He threw his hands up in the air and pushed the chair back, going to stand at the window. 'That's it now, I give up.'

Annie was shocked at his words, more so as she thought she'd never hear them come from him. She walked slowly up behind him, reaching up to put her hands on his shoulders. She squeezed them, then turned him to face her.

'You're not seeing things as they really are at the moment Kit. Yes. You've had plenty of setbacks but don't think for a minute that the village doesn't want what you want. I've only been in this village for five minutes and you may think it's not my place to comment. Yet I've seen their faces at the meeting – eager and hopeful. I've heard them in the village and at the library talking proudly about 'their Stone' The excitement at the pub that they might be able to hold a festival up there. They are a great community anyway but this 'belonging' connected with the stone really cements that community together. You are their only hope Kit so please don't give up. Remember your own words at the meeting – 'It is our history and our heritage - and it needs to be reclaimed.'

Kit stared at her for a few moments as she watched his eyes change from unbearably sad to questioning until finally, they crinkled up with warmth and he pulled her up to him, her head resting on his chest.

'Thank you Annie, I needed that. A swift kick up the backside. You can come and give me some home truths anytime you want.' Then he kissed the top of her head gently.

Annie stood back quickly while wondering why on earth she wasn't staying nestling into his chest, smelling the clean smell of lemon on his clothes and wanting to tilt her head up so he didn't have to kiss the top of her head. She mumbled that she had to get back and then pulled Chess out, leaving Kit staring after her, lost in thought.

Chapter 21

Kit popped down to Annie's later that day to apologise for using her as a confessor but she said that he could confess anytime he wanted.

'Thanks but no thanks. That's it now' he said No more getting fired up over the Stone.'

'You don't mean you *are* giving up do you?'

'No, just stepping back a bit, taking things a bit more calmly and not letting it take over my life. I'm overseeing an ongoing project in the Highlands so I'll go up and have a look at that after tonight. I like to spend March 21st or thereabouts in proximity to the Stone. There you go again; it *is* taking over my life.

Annie laughed and then asked, 'March 21st? Start of Spring. Is that a solstice too?'

'No it's the Spring or vernal equinox. Basically the Summer and Winter solstices are when the sun is at its furthest point from the earth, hence the longest day and the shortest day. The Spring and Autumn equinox is when the sun is directly overhead and the days and nights are equal in length.'

'So – are you a pagan then Kit?' she asked, seeing as the village was beginning to appear like a throwback to the Middle Ages.

'I'm not anything in particular. I go my own way and do what I want. If I want to go to church, I will. If I want to enjoy the magic of standing stones, I will. It's the history and traditions I love – but I respect those who think otherwise.

He thought for a minute.

'Why don't you come up and watch the sun rise at the Stone in the morning?'

'What unearthly time would that be?' she said calmly although she wanted to shout 'YES!'

'About six am. but we should arrive a little earlier to get the full effect. That's if there is a sun, it's given fog on the weather forecast.'

'Oh it *must* be right then if the weather forecast says so' she grinned, thinking of the inconsistencies of the forecasts.

Kit laughed and said he'd meet her outside his house at 5.30 am. in the morning.

*

So here she was, wrapped up in a woolly hat, scarf, gloves, boots and two jumpers as well as her parka with the hood pulled up. She was just turning into Kit's lane. She had brought Chess with her and just hoped that all three dogs didn't start barking at this early hour. Luckily they seemed subdued by the almost-darkness, which was made worse by the predicted fog. Annie had to admit it made everything seem spooky. Even Kit's lovely house looked like the Addam's Family mansion, looming out of the swirling mists.

Kit had his long coat and his leather hat on, which he tipped towards her in greeting. When they had walked a little further up the lane, he said softly,

'We may have company up there you know.'

Annie shuddered, visions of shadowy figures appearing from behind the Stone.

'You mean the souls of your ancestors?' she whispered.

There was a muted explosion next to her that sounded suspiciously like a laugh.

'I was thinking more of Minerva Jones.'

'Oh. Yes. And maybe Marje from the pub?'

'No, I think Marje is a sort of house-witch. She celebrates the Summer festivals but won't brave the cold for anything like this. She does do candle-burning ceremonies at home to celebrate though. She also reads the Tarot cards and picks herbs from her garden but I don't think the Stone has as much significance in that way for her. It does mean a lot to her as a born and bred villager though. She's more of a hobby-witch – and if she heard me say that, she'd turn me into a frog if she could! Besides, like she's fond of saying, she's the 'only witch in the village' and it's not much fun on your own.

'Min manages by herself though' said Annie.

'She takes her duties as a Druid far more seriously, as did most of her family before her.' replied Kit. 'She respects Nature and wants to celebrate it on these special days. The Stone is very important to her.'

They strolled up quietly then, while watching the sky begin to lighten in thin strips of mauve against the retreating blackness. The fog had dispersed until there was just a mist throwing a gossamer-thin veil over everything. As they skirted round the wood, they looked east to see that the sky was opening up and a watery sun was just making an appearance over the horizon. They turned back and saw the Stone, silhouetted against the sky. A little further on, Kit put his finger to his lips and stopped dead in front of her, pulling her into the woods.

Is this my lucky day? thought Annie, smiling to herself before he pointed out a kneeling figure at the far side of the Stone who had been hidden by it on the way up. In a voluminous white cloak and hood, she was instantly recognisable as Min. She was kneeling down on the ground, looking towards the sun rising in the east with her hands held up above her in supplication as the orb rose over the horizon and became stronger.

They both stayed in the woods silently, the dogs following their example as if they had read his mind. When Annie turned to her right, they could see the sun rising in Min's line of sight. Kit bent down and whispered in her ear.

'Follow me further up the wood. We can see it better without disturbing her' and they crept up to a place where they were still hidden but could see the stone from a point behind Min now.

Annie was mesmerised. The Winterfell Stone stood dark against the lightening sky, the mellow sun striking across the top of the Stone and illuminating the tiny crystalline specks. The remaining mist made it look otherworldly. There was a stillness about the place, as though the world was holding its breath. Even the birds were still silent.

Then there was a low growl from the throat of Chess, who had never growled as long as she'd lived with Annie. The other dog's ears pricked up. Suddenly, from further up in the wood, two men broke cover. One had a shotgun in his hands and the other held a snarling dog on a chain. They all ran over towards Min and before she, Kit or Annie had realised what was happening, they had grabbed her and were hauling her back towards the lane.

Before Annie had time to process anything, Kit shot out of the woods towards the figures.

'Gardman – release her now!' he shouted in such a commanding voice that one man immediately did as he was told. The other, obviously Gardman, shouted back.

'You keep out of this Courtney. You're not Lord of the Manor now you know, telling us what to do. This woman, aside from performing ungodly practices, is trespassing on my land. I am escorting her from it and defending it with this' he jerked up the rifle in one hand. 'I'm also reporting her to the police for trespass. I've had enough of her sneaking onto my land. I've had enough of you all. You heathen worshippers of false gods. This'll teach you. I'll do the same to anyone I catch here. Dick is now on regular patrol with Nero and he's got every right to set him on anyone who hasn't permission to be on this land.'

'I said – let her go' continued Kit as though the farmer hadn't spoken. His voice was firm and full of authority. Annie could see Gardman wavering then he dropped Min's arm. A sob escaped her as she dropped to the floor.

'Get her off my land then and I've warned you – keep away. All of you. And I'm still reporting her for trespass.'

Annie watched as Kit gently eased Min to a standing position and with his arm round her shoulders, started to lead her towards the path. Annie saw her face - devastated, embarrassed – with tears rolling down her face. Before she knew it she was standing in front of Gardman.

'And you' she spat 'you are as ungodly as your supposedly Christian friend the ex-Reverend. What is wrong with letting her or anyone else come to look at the Stone. They don't harm your land. You don't do anything with it anyway, it's full of bumps and mounds. People can't harm it just by being here. Where is your sense of community, connection with your fellow men? Where is the milk of human kindness? You're more ungodly than any of us here.'

At this, Gardman's face darkened and he took a step towards her. Even Dick looked worried. She saw Kit and Min frozen in time, their eyes wide and Kit dropped Min's arm in readiness.

Annie though, was made of strong stuff and instead of backing off, she took a step towards him instead, bringing them face to face. She leant in,

'If you report her for trespass, I'll report you to the police for threatening behaviour and issuing verbal threats on Mr Courtney's private land.'

Gardman looked around him as if just registering that he had brought Min onto the edge of the lane. Kit's private road.

'I'm also going to report you to the Right to Roam association and the Human Rights commission -and the Village Hall committee' she finished lamely, then strode off as Kit and Min followed.

*

Thawing out back at Kit's with a cup of hot sweet tea in her hand, the colour had come back to Min's cheeks.

'I'm never going to go up there again. In fact I don't know why I'm still a Druid as we are constantly maligned and misunderstood. I don't ever want to go through that again.'

'Minerva Jones' said Kit quietly 'I didn't have you down as a quitter. What you do doesn't affect anyone else and there's no harm in it whether you believe in it or not. I know it's your connection and feel for Nature as well as tradition that keeps you remaining as a Druid. If you give that up, then Gardman has won hasn't he?'

Min didn't say anything but gave him a flicker of a smile.

'Well I've been called a scarlet woman in church so you can be scarlet woman number two and join me. ' added Annie. 'You say you're misunderstood? What if you explain to people and they might understand more than you think?

Kit smiled and nodded as Min shrugged her shoulders.

'Maybe' she said, sounding unsure 'but can I say again a huge thank you to you both. I don't know what would have happened if you hadn't been there.'

'Nothing' said Kit 'Like all bullies he's all talk and no action – the gun was a prop and the dog was for show. Although he might still report you for trespass as we all know how vindictive he is. That's unless Annie has scared the hell out of him.'

'You were magnificent Annie, the way you stood up to him' Min looked up at her gratefully while Kit smiled and added.

'And gave him the mother of all lectures. Even your lecture in the church when you first arrived was very calm but I've never seen you hopping mad like that.'

Kit and Min exchanged glances then very unexpectedly burst out laughing. Annie was glad Min was actually laughing – but not that she was laughing at her. She felt a little affronted. Kit stopped for a minute and said,

'I wondered what else you were going to find to report him to as well as the Village Hall committee?'

Annie's mouth twitched. Kit went on mercilessly.

'You only missed out the Booker Prize committee and the Tufty Club!'

At this both he and Min doubled over with laughter, probably brought on with relief more than anything and this time Annie joined in. When they eventually stopped and Min and her were getting up to go, she turned to look at Kit.

'Do you think it's worth telling the Tufty Club though? They might help?'

'Go home Millford' he grinned.

DIARY

I really thought I'd turned a corner. I felt as though I'd been accepted here after five years. More to do with my attitude than anything else I suppose.

I was joining in with the Stone Circle group and on various committees in the village. Acceptance, for someone like me who has always been on the outside looking in, is so very important.

I was quite pleased with my appearance as I've lost a bit of weight. Percy seems to be paying me a bit more attention too although I expect he still sees me as nothing more than a friend.

Then this! Total humiliation. I know Kit and Annie won't say a word but nothing ever stays secret in a village. I don't know how my being a Druid has stayed secret for this long although some people may have guessed. The trusted ones that do know - they won't breathe a word.

Will Farmer Gardman keep it to himself? Will he hell! If he knew how to use a mobile phone and had taken a photo of me, it would have been printed and handed to the local paper or pinned on the village noticeboard by now. Luckily, he thinks mobile phones are the work of the Devil so at least I'm spared that.

Dick Eastley, one of his farmworkers was there too. He wouldn't have dared disobey his boss when they caught me. He's not a bad man really but he'll tell Ginny Eastley, she'll tell the W.I. and I'll be thrown out of it - never to darken their door again. I'll be ejected from all the other committees too, the Village Hall committee, May Day committee, maybe even the Stone Circle although most of them already know what I am.

The worst thing is it's my fault. No one else to blame. One half of me thinks that maybe I should have learnt to conform by now. Try not to be different. I haven't got the personality to bring off 'different'. I like to melt into the background and not bring attention to myself, though how being a Druid quite equates with that part of my character I don't know.

Yet the other half of me thinks that Kit was right - and Annie in her church 'lecture' before Christmas - that we should be allowed to follow what faith we want without others sitting in judgement on us. I hope I have the courage to go on believing this.

Annie hit the nail on the head saying that I should try and explain about modern day Druids who only practice rituals eight times a year. They don't have weekly meetings and don't have a universal text like the Bible or the Koran. They don't curse your livestock and make them barren either...

People in general have the wrong idea . It is based on the Natural world and sacrifices and devil worship are as far away from the truth as they can be. How can I explain this though? Knock on their doors? Rattle a few leaflets out on the printer? Do I really want to lay my whole life bare for them?

And Percy. Oh dear god Percy. He knows what I am in theory I think, although he has never discussed it - but the embarrassment of when it becomes a reality, not just something that isn't spoken about. He is a shy man, conventional in many ways. Will he still want to be my friend when the grapevine starts growing and my 'citizen's arrest' becomes widely known?

I shall just have to accept whatever comes my way. I hope I shan't have to leave again. This is the longest I've stayed in one place and I am so fond of this village. And the people. Most of them...

Talking of which - Kit and Annie. Kit has always been a fine young man as long as I've known him. High principles and doesn't suffer fools gladly ; slightly eccentric but then who am I to talk? Yet he is one of the kindest, most generous, most loyal people I know, with a wicked sense of humour to boot. I could speak to him about anything and there have been times when I have, and I know he'd listen. He's called me inside when I've passed his house if I've looked miserable - which was most of the time. He's said he is always there if anything is troubling me and because he has endless patience, I've taken him up on that rather too often.

Annie - what can I say? How wrong could I have been? I'm a fine one to talk about people judging me when I judged her so harshly from the first minute I met her. Of course, I realise I may have been jealous of her looks, her carefree attitude and her ability to make friends with people straight away. She didn't appear to flap when a houseful of people invaded her home unexpectedly. What about the way - and I think I always knew what she was doing subconsciously - that she gently pushed me towards Percy with hints and practical help.

If I wasn't already firmly in her camp, today would have done it. She leapt to my defence against Gardman like a tigress. That was the action of a true friend. I think Kit was impressed too. What IS going on there? Anything? Who knows, especially with Kit, who is a law unto himself.

Writing it down in my diary has been cathartic, so I will just wait and see the reactions when the gossip starts. I hope I can sleep tonight-because, as another Scarlet(t) woman *said - 'Tomorrow is another day'. And thank heavens for that!*

Chapter 22

The library had only been opened for five minutes before Min was saying it was her fault that no one was coming in. It was the first time it had been open since the 'incident'. Annie tried to reassure her that she was blowing it up out of all proportion in her mind and nobody would have even have heard a thing about it. The vicar walked in.

'Good morning to you ladies' she boomed. 'I've heard about what happened…'Min gave Annie a sidelong glance through narrowed eyes. 'and I just want to say I thought it was absolutely disgusting.'

Min's shoulders sagged.

'That awful farmer's treatment of you ought to be reported. He was boasting about it in the newsagents and it sounded like assault to me. I've come to see if you're alright?' Cynthia put her hand on Min's shoulder as her lips began to quiver.

'Mr Clegg who owns the newsagent gave him 'what for' too. Said he was a bully. To his face. Now, to the business in hand. Have you got any new, gory, bloodthirsty thrillers you can recommend? You know the type I like.'

Annie took her to the Gory and Bloodthirsty section while Min composed herself. She turned round and stuck her tongue out at her in an 'I told you so' gesture.

Mr Cartwright appeared ten minutes later. Annie was going through to check on the I.T. room but stood back when she saw him at the other side of the glass doors. He still seemed a little nervous when he saw her. He entered through the open door but still gave her a wide berth even though she was standing stock still but at least he had a smile on his face now. Annie hung back a little as he went to the counter.

'I've just brought these back Miss Jones, and I have to say...'

Min froze and Annie held her breath.

'…that this is a free country and you should be allowed to do what you want, within reason of course – and folks shouldn't gossip about it so I won't say any more. I've said my piece. I've never liked that farmer though. Now, have you got those books I reserved.?'

This went on all morning. Even if they weren't sure what Min was actually doing up there or what she actually was, it didn't matter in the grand scheme of things because they all actively disliked Gardman. Mostly though, the ones who did know everything had an encouraging word for her.

'Oh no' gasped Min, wide-eyed and staring out of the window at a smart lady with immaculate hair and clothes. 'The local school headmistress. Mrs Knight. I was going to help out with May Day celebrations at the school. She'll be here to tell me she doesn't want the children associated with any so-called Pagan goings-on.'

'Your glass has been half empty for so long, what's left has evaporated.' Annie told her but she did look worried as an efficient-looking Mrs Knight click-clacked across the floor in her power heels.

'Miss Jones' she said. Min had a rictus grin plastered on her face and her top lip was sweating.

'Mrs Knight' she said in a wobbly voice.

'I've just popped in during my break, can't be long but you know you'd said you'd assist us with May Day celebrations at the school?'

'Mmff' snuffled Min, gripping the edge of the counter.

'Well I wondered if it would be possible to scrap that idea?'

'Yes, yes, I see, of course, although I, yes well. It wasn't, you know anything that…Well I'm sorry that you want - of course, your prerogative, but – yes, yes, it's, of course, it's, I understand…'

Min had caught the verbal diarrhoea train and didn't want to get off, until Annie walked behind her and nudged her back as she passed. Mrs Knight looked slightly taken aback but pressed on, leaning in confidentially.

'I was wondering if we could hold the school celebrations at the Winterfell Stone instead? I know Professor Courtney had mentioned village festivals up there and perhaps by then it might be alright? Or perhaps if I ask the farmer, he won't be able to refuse as it involves the whole school? For the community spirit I mean?'

Mrs Knight looked from Min – who had her mouth open – to Annie, whose eyebrows were raised so high they threatened to disappear into her hairline. Mrs Knight pressed on regardless.

'I'd heard he was a bit funny with you which I don't approve of but I thought if we both asked him together? Miss Jones?'

Min's mouth was so wide now that she resembled one of those painted faces at the fair where you throw ping-pong balls into their mouths and win a fish. Annie shook her head to dispel the thought and answered for her.

'Have you actually met Mr Gardman, the farmer?' she asked.

'I'm afraid not. I live in Axeholme so I don't know too many local people, other than the school steering committee and some of the parents of course.' Mrs Knight replied with a smile.

'Well, when you heard he was a bit funny with Minerva, we're talking shotguns and vicious dogs here.' The headmistresses eyes opened wide. 'and when you say, "he won't be able to refuse", I'm here to tell you that he most certainly will refuse and will follow it up by saying that you and every child in the school will be going to hell for celebrating Pagan festivals and will finish it off by shouting "AND KEEP OFF MY LAND!"'

Annie swallowed hard then looked at Min.

'Isn't that right?'

'That's about the size of it' replied Min 'and Annie got his predictable responses down to a T.'

'Oh my goodness, I didn't realise how things were or I wouldn't even have asked. I've obviously only heard half the story. Well, we won't be demeaning ourselves by asking such an awful man, Miss Jones. I've got to get back but perhaps we can meet in the Hunter's Moon pub on the corner around 5.30 pm? Then you can tell me the real story. You too Miss Millford? You'll still help me at the school on May Day though won't you? With your credentials, you'd be perfect. And there's that other project I'd like to talk about regarding the herb garden, we only skirted it last time?'

'I'd love to. *We'd* love to' breathed Min, with obvious relief on her face as she checked with Annie.

'Good, I'll see you both there' said Mrs Knight as she swept out on a cloud of Light Blue by Dolce and Gabbana.

'Told you' Annie grinned at Min who had slowly crumpled and put her head on the counter.

'She's actually a very nice lady but I felt like I'd been caught smoking at school then.' Min sighed.

At lunchtime, Min told Annie it was time she went home. She was a lot brighter now as more people had come in and given her a vote of confidence. In fact, the library had never been so busy with people coming in, even if they didn't hold a library card, just to say they sided with Min.

'It's only because they dislike Gardman so much' she said.

'Do you think, Min-the-eternal-pessimist, that it could possibly be because they like you|?'

Min coloured up and looked pleased, then noticed the clock. 'Go on, get yourself off, Chess will be behind the door checking her watch!' Min laughed.

'Actually, I was wondering if I could have a look at those old reference books in the cupboard before I go?'

Min looked surprised but went for the key. The ancient-looking tomes were kept in a locked cupboard that used to stand in the original library building and was now at the back of the librarian's inner sanctum, along with a small table, two uncomfortable chairs and a kettle.

She unlocked the cupboard without enquiring as to why. She knew there would be a good reason and Annie would tell her if she needed to know. She had shown it to her when she started, describing it as a cupboard full of old books that no one wants any more. Well obviously Annie did. They had probably been transferred from Huntingdon Hall many years ago when Kit's grandfather sold it the building. It was obviously not wanted by his son at the Lodge.

As Min returned to the library, Annie pulled out a heavy book, the one she remembered seeing on her first day here. It didn't mean much at the time but more recent events had brought it back to mind. She pulled it out and lugged it over to the table. Inscribed in gold letters on the leather spine was 'The Estate, tenants, land and sundry farm buildings of Huntingdon Hall'

Annie carefully turned over the discoloured pages. On the title page, it showed it had been written in 1783. Further on, she read the Hall had been built in 1682, replacing an earlier manor house. She read an account of the cottages belonging to tenant farm workers. It mentioned the row of three cottages where she now lived. They must have been part of the original estate back then.

Annie examined a map on the next page which was covered with a page of what looked like tracing paper. It showed the cottages, which weren't named but were in the right position, which comprised Bank Farm terrace. Bank Farm must have been the tenanted farm the cottage residents worked for.

A few pages on, another map showed Kit's house or an earlier version, still called Hunter's

Lodge. It showed the ancient woodland too. Annie leaned in closer and then checked if the maps were to scale. Perhaps not totally accurate but hopefully accurate enough, thought Annie, her heart beating faster. She took out her mobile and took photos of the map and of a few paragraphs preceding it.

Annie handed back the key and rushed off back to Chess. Kit was up in the Highlands and wasn't back till Saturday. She would wait till then and just pray she wouldn't be giving him false hope.

Chapter 23

Chess was hanging around Annie, not letting her out of her sight. Every way she turned, she tripped over the ever-present dog who was practicing her best 'I'm being abandoned' looks. She knew something was going on.

In fact, Annie was only going to be away for the day. She was going to meet her publisher in Skipton to talk about 'Chessie the Rescue Dog'. The woman had already seen Lettie in Edinburgh and was now on her way to Skipton to meet Annie before she returned to the London headquarters. Lettie had phoned last night but refused to divulge any details apart from it definitely wasn't bad news. Annie wondered if they were going to ask her to change some of the illustrations – although looking down at Chess now, Annie thought she'd caught the pathetic, sympathy-seeking expression perfectly. She laughed and bent down to ruffle the little dog's ears.

'It's okay you silly dog, I'll be back soon and you're staying with your favourite babysitter.'

Maisie had started having Chess over at hers when Annie did her two stints at the library. She said it was company for her and indeed, the two of them got on very well. Chess was always impeccably behaved when she was there, curling up on the hearth rug and occasionally going for her head stroked. When Annie collected her, she just stayed where she was and opened one eye to let her know she wasn't that excited about coming home. As soon as Annie made for Maisie's door though, she was off like a shot. She may love Maisie but Annie and her adopted sheepdog had a special bond.

Annie dropped her off today with a warning for Maisie to ignore her if she begged for food as she would be back before her teatime. Walking to the station, she noticed Gavin and Wendy outside the vets, talking to Cynthia. Those two, once they had stopped playing at silly devils, had become a firm couple. She wondered whether talking to the vicar could indicate a wedding was on the cards and then realised she was getting the village mentality of thinking that she knew everybody's business.

The train was crowded and it was a warm day so she was glad she had opted for the plain white shift dress under her navy jacket although she would be trying to keep it clean all day. She tried to avoid getting chocolate on it now as she bit into a mint aero. She hadn't had breakfast as they would be having an early lunch meeting but her stomach was rumbling already and she just happened to have this bar in her bag. Other people have emergency tissues, spare cash or Swiss army knives; she had chocolate.

The Romano Bistro was on a cobbled side street. It had flowers outside and a striped canopy advertising the name. Luckily, she had met Simone Ellerker before so she knew who she was looking for. As she entered the place, a small, red-haired whirlwind threw herself at Lettie,

'Anniiiee!' she screamed, startling the few early diners at the tables.

'Lettie! What on earth are you doing here?' said Annie in amazement, she was a long way from home.

'Well that's a fine greeting from my best friend I must say' huffed Lettie, spoiling it with a grin.

'Oh no, I mean I'm so pleased to see you obviously but…'

'Simone is taking me back to London with her to meet the publishers. All expenses paid. I told her to stipulate the Ritz but apparently they laughed. No one ever takes me seriously.'

Lettie had been the livewire joker at school whereas Annie was more the knuckling-down, studious type. They both got the same amount of GCSEs and A levels though so either Lettie was one of those people who didn't have to try – or it said something about taking life too seriously. A lesson Annie hadn't learnt soon enough but was now trying to make up for. They were both creative though and their sense of humour drew them together and until Lettie met her future husband and moved to Scotland, they had seen each other every week. They still tried to meet at least twice a year.

'Please sit down and order what you want' said Simone 'it's all expenses paid here too. It may not be the Ritz but…'

'It's lovely' replied Annie looking around, The mouth-watering smells coming from the kitchen were tantalising and she grabbed the menu in anticipation. She ordered Fettuccine Alfredo while Lettie ordered a bottle of good red wine.

'Well, if it's on our publisher's account, why not?' she laughed 'and we're not driving anyway'

She suddenly remembered Simone *was* driving and looked at her apologetically. Simone laughed.

'Don't you worry about me; I prefer champagne anyway.'

'Wooh!' Annie and Lettie turned the sarcasm on in unison.

'Although I doubt we'll manage the whole bottle between ourselves' said Annie.

'You're forgetting when I lived at Cambersea, that would have just been with our starters' Lettie replied, raising an eyebrow.

'We're older and wiser though now aren't we?' answered Annie.

'We're older anyway' laughed Lettie.

Over a lengthy meal, Simone managed to reveal - despite Lettie squeaking and telling her to hurry up whilst bouncing in her seat- that Broome and Banner, publishers, wanted to commission a series of four 'Chessie the Recue Dog' books. There was an option for more if they were well received, which was anticipated as the firm had loved the concept, the illustrations and the story.

This was fantastic news for Annie as it meant she didn't have to worry about finances this year now as she knew she would have this money to fall back on.

'A toast' smiled Simone, holding her glass of tonic water up and the waitress stepped forward to top up the other glasses.

Somehow, and she couldn't picture it later, Annie flung her arm out to pick up her glass and nudged the waitress's arm, changing the flow of the wine from into the glass, to onto the front of her clean white dress. There was a pause as the whole restaurant seemed to hold its breath, then Annie started to giggle as her companions stared at each other in amazement. Then she threw her head back and started laughing.

'Are you hysterical?' asked Lettie, genuinely concerned. 'Should I slap you?'

'I'm so sorry ' whispered the young waitress, glancing nervously towards the kitchens, 'It was all my fault. I'll pay for the dress to be dry cleaned.'

Annie swallowed and straightened her face. 'It was *not* your fault; it was totally mine. I can throw the dress away when I get home as it cost less than five pounds from a charity shop. I might need something to cover me up till I get there though, this jacket is too low at the front.'

'I'll find you something' said the young girl gratefully and thank you. I really need this job.

Lettie was staring at her. 'You've changed' she said simply.

'You think?'

'Yes because the Annie I knew would have got so stressed out over that incident. You wouldn't have blamed the girl still but you would have beaten yourself up over it and wondered what people would think. But…you laughed!' she said incredulously.

'It is strange' agreed Annie. 'Since I decided that enough was enough with my teaching, unpaid overtime, tutoring, volunteering and committee work, I think I have changed. It was like an epiphany. From that very moment, nothing seemed to matter as much as it did before. Suddenly all the tension melted away. I've become prone to clumsiness-witness the wine- I seem to have a lack of tact where I was Miss Diplomatic but I'm definitely not stressed anymore.'

'You do seem less serious, is that what you mean?' asked Lettie while trying to mop up Annie's dress with red paper serviettes and making it worse.

Annie paused for a moment.

'How's this? Within a week of moving to Winterfell, I mistook a man picking his wife up from the station for a taxi driver and asked for a lift. I inadvertently called an eminent professor a tramp and then, inadvertently again, nearly mowed him down as I sledged down the snowy lane to the village.'

The other two burst out laughing. 'That'll do! I love it' chuckled Lettie. 'Who are you and what have you done with Annie Millford?'

At that moment the waitress arrived with a nervous and apologetic expression on her face.

'I'm afraid this is all I could find' and she held up a black t-shirt which would cover up the wine but would proclaim her as an employee of Romano's, which was written all over the front.

Annie took the proffered cover-up, thanking the girl and reassuring the waiter who was hovering behind her that it was genuinely not the girl's fault at all. She didn't want her getting into trouble.

After saying tearful goodbyes to her friend and giving Simone a hug, she made her way towards the station. She checked the time. If she didn't make this train in less than ten minutes, she had another two hours to wait. She walked on to the station and seeing Marje on the platform, told her eagerly of the new 'Chessie' series of books.

'That's great news' said Marje' but also disappointing.'

'Disappointing? Why?' asked Annie hesitantly.

'Because I was just going to order the vegetable lasagne with garlic bread' Marje replied, nodding at the top Annie had forgotten she was wearing.

'That's off today but we have a delicious pasta Puttanesca' laughed Annie and told her the story on the way home.

Chapter 24

They arrived at Winterfell station having discussed every subject under the sun, including the best spell for making a man fall in love with you.

'I make a potion infused with certain herbs for that reason too' Marje had said. 'I'm looking for an opportunity to slip some in Minerva Jones' tea sometime.'

Poor Min. Was it so obvious to everyone about her feelings towards Percy? Annie wasn't sure it was even obvious to Min and it certainly wasn't to Percy. Marje had assured her too that everyone who had discussed Min's 'incident' at the Stone - this was a village after all so that probably meant the entire population – was on her side.

'Try telling that to Min' Annie had said. 'However much I tell her that, she's still convinced she's going to be tarred and feathered, then drummed out of the village, never to taint their streets again.

As they got off the train, Frank's wife got on and they exchanged greetings. Outside, Frank was just about to get into Adrian's taxi when he saw Annie.

'Good afternoon, m'lady' he said in a perfect, sinus-afflicted Parker the Chauffeur voice as he opened the rear door.

'Good afternoon Parker' Annie replied in a cut-glass Lady Penelope voice. 'If it's not too much trouble?'

'Not at all, m'lady'

'But you only live up the road' said Marje, unintentionally joining in the impressions with a 'You're as mad as a box of frogs' voice.'

'When you have delicate little tootsies like mine, you shouldn't have to walk far.' Annie now seemed to be morphing into Queenie from Blackadder. 'Besides, I don't want anyone else ordering an Italian meal from me on the way home.'

'So, no pizza for my trouble then?' Frank winked as Annie and Marje got in the car.

'I quite like being driven by a plumber with a split personality' she grinned as Marje shook her head in bemusement.

Frank first dropped Marje at the pub then Annie up the lane.

'At least let me get you a cup of tea and a biscuit or two?' smiled Annie.

'No thanks, I'm going back home to play the trumpet in peace for a couple of hours while the wife's out so she can't complain. Cheerio'

Annie waved him off wondering whether the words 'in peace' were really relevant in this case? Or whether Adrian next door might complain instead of Frank's wife?

She opened the gate of the passageway between her and Ada's and went straight round to Maisie's back door to collect Chess. The dog was down at the bottom of Maisie's garden but soon bounded up as soon as she heard Annie call. Maisie poked her head out of her back door.

'Good news or bad news?'

'Very good. They're asking for enough illustrations for another three books after this one, so that will keep me going for a while.

'I'm very pleased love' said Maisie. 'Is it warm enough out there to eat outside?'

It was, Annie told her, but they might need a coat. So Annie went to fetch hers, change her clothes and feed Chess while Maisie brought a huge tray of food out and put it on the little table outside her kitchen window.

'I've made us some tea, not too much as I know you've had a big lunch. I asked Ada and Tom but they're finishing off a chicken that needs eating today. They might join us for a cuppa after though. Can we borrow your two plastic chairs?

'Of course' and Annie placed them at the other side of the table. She shouldn't be hungry at all but she was surprised at how much her mouth was watering at the sandwiches; egg mayonnaise in brown and ham in white, then scones with jam and fresh cream. She had been eating much more since she'd lived here. She hadn't had much time to eat at Cambersea, just grabbing a bite to eat when she could. She should have been putting weight on now but had stayed the same, mainly due to eating a better diet now she had time to make food and to walking Chess every day.

She relaxed back in the chair, chatting to Maisie and drinking in the fields and the dales beyond. The sun still had some warmth in it and the nights were getting lighter. There was a line of pale mauve hanging over the hills, not long before it started getting dark now. She would have to sort out those pots for the garden sometime soon – and the veg for the box down at the bottom. She had got as far as ringing the letting agent to ask about digging a flower bed along the length of the path but he had been doubtful, so she'd decided to leave it for now. She could still make it a nice place to sit in and look at her garden and the views beyond in the coming summer. Then she could have her neighbours round for afternoon tea in the garden to repay them for their kindness.

Right on cue, Ada and Tom arrived. They sat in Annie's plastic chairs and they all immediately started catching up on the village gossip. Annie wondered if they discussed her? Of course they would but none of them had malicious tongues. It was all ordinary, everyday stuff and she was pleased that Min wasn't the subject of discussion, although that was probably old news by now. If only Min herself could believe that. Min's confidence, just when it was gaining strength, had hit rock bottom again.

Tom leant forward. 'I've got some lettuce seedlings for you and some spring onion ones too. And some seed potatoes for the sack I gave you. I'll have a couple of tomato plants for you too but I'll keep'em in my greenhouse for now. I was thinking, if you want to get one of those mini lean-to greenhouses, I'll have a lot more for you. You'll never have to buy a tomato till October.'

'He's determined to make a veg grower out of you lass' laughed Ada 'he failed dismally with me.'

'Aye but you like eating the produce don't you?' grinned Tom 'even if you're the kiss of death for any plant.' He turned back to Annie.

'We'll soon have you sorted. I can come round and show you how to plant them if you'd like?'

It was on the tip of Annie's tongue to say she wouldn't put him to the bother before she realised that he loved to help and pass on his knowledge. It was his personal mission to make her a gardener.

'I'd love that Tom' she smiled. 'Thank you.'

The others went back inside and Annie thanked Maisie, helping her wash up and clear away. She put the chairs back outside her cottage and sat down for a few minutes. The hills and fields were dark now and Chess was just a moving shape trotting up and down the garden until she eventually came and nuzzled Annie's hand. They went inside, Annie turning for one last look at the deep purple sky and the red glow over the hills.

Chapter 25

It was now just over a week before the village May Day celebrations, to be held on the school field. There would be Maypole dancing by the children, organised by Min and stalls selling local produce, books and plants. There was also a hoop-la stall and a hook-a-duck. The most popular would probably be a stall where the children had the chance to throw a wet sponge at two of their teachers. The children were also running a raffle and a tombola too. The posters for this event were all around the village but this morning, Annie and Chess were going round the shops and businesses with a smaller set of adverts reminding people of the May Day committee meeting. This would finalise the details and make sure everyone had their instructions. This would normally be for the May Day committee only but Annie had seen Min scribbling away over the pile of papers and now noticed they had 'Public Meeting' written across them in marker pen. Min had personally asked each member of the Stone Circle to be there too. She had looked enquiringly at Min who stayed tight-lipped and looked away. Annie knew better than to pursue the matter   She and Chess were now making their way back down the village street having delivered the notices. She was desperate to tell Kit her news but would wait till tomorrow when she could see him in person. Marje was outside the Hunter's Moon, watering the hanging baskets. She stopped Annie pointing to one of the notices now in her window, asking her if she knew what it was about. Chess gladly had a drink from the water bowl next to the entrance.

What happened next remained a blur in Annie's memory. Kit was across the road, back a day early and talking to Gavin. He saw Annie and went to the edge of the pavement, ready to cross over to her. Unfortunately, just at that moment, Chess looked up and saw her second-favourite person in the whole world and threw the 'intelligent sheepdog' tag off by making a mad dash to see Kit, pulling the lead out of Annie's hand.

She only later remembered a roar to her left where a motorbike was pulling out of her lane and heading right, into the village.

'CHESS!' she shouted and lunged forwards, knowing in her heart she would be too late. The next thing she remembered seeing, as if in a dream, was Kit diving for the terrified dog who had suddenly realised the danger and had frozen to the spot.

He scooped her up and made for Annie at high speed but the motorbike, although desperately braking, hit him a glancing blow before slewing across the road.

Kit had released Chess, who was now shaking like a leaf next to Annie, but her rescuer was now spread out on the road with his eyes closed.

Annie screamed and ran to him while Marje grabbed hold of Chess's lead and stroked and hugged the trembling but otherwise unharmed dog.

'Kit, Kit! Say something!' shouted Annie as she bent down to the prone figure lying as still as a statue.

After what seemed hours to Annie but was probably only seconds, one of his eyes cautiously opened.

'Ow?' he suggested in response.

'Oh god! I thought you were dead. Does it hurt anywhere?'

'Yes' he said, opening the other eye to look at her anxious face.

'Well WHERE?' she didn't mean to shout but he might have broken something.

'I don't think I've broken anything' he croaked as though reading her mind, 'my leg hurts, my side...'

'Don't move, I'm trained in First Aid' squeaked Annie in a quivering falsetto and started gently feeling up and down his leg. The corner of Kit's mouth twitched but he didn't dare say anything.

'Tell me if it hurts.'

'It hurts'

'You're a man of few words today Kit Courtney.' She was getting disproportionately annoyed with his glib answers, not taking account of him being flat out in the road.

'Well I'm sorry, Nurse Millford, but I didn't feel like giving a speech with the whole village looking on.'

At this, Annie turned and saw what actually looked like most of the village, congregating around them and looking on with concern. More people were hurrying from different directions. Kit eased himself into a half-sitting position and

Gavin asked him to wiggle his toes before he helped him up and onto the pavement.

'If I were a horse, would you shoot me?' he laughed and Gavin said no, but he'd have to cut back on the hay for a while, which set them both off laughing.

'I'm glad you think it's FUNNY!' shouted Annie 'You could have been killed and it's all my fault. I wasn't holding the lead tight enough' and she promptly burst into tears.

Kit tried to put an arm round her shoulders but winced instead.

'I think you'll find it's my fault. Didn't see the dog till the last second. Tried to stop but…' The motorbike rider had come over and joined the blame game.

'It was a simple accident' said Kit, 'are you alright?'

'Thanks mate – and I'm fine. Bit shaken but not as bad as you must be. How's the dog?'

They all turned towards a very sorry-looking Chess who was trying her best to look innocent coupled with extreme repentance.

'What's the best thing for shock in dogs Gavin?' asked Kit, looking worried.

'Lots of cuddles, which she seems to be getting.'

Annie had gone across and was talking to her in a calming voice. She knew Chess would be okay when she licked her on her nose and sniffed her pocket for treats. In the distance an ambulance siren could be heard. Kit looked annoyed.

'Who called an ambulance?' he said 'nobody is badly hurt , it's pointless dragging them away from something more serious.'

'I did' confessed Trevor. 'It looked bad to me through the pub window and I didn't want to take a chance.'

'Quite right Trev – and shut up Kit. You need to be checked out' said Marje.

'I really don't' grumbled Kit.

By this time the ambulance had pulled up next to them, dispersing the crowd of people. They had been en route back to base so had diverted here quickly. Once they had ascertained that the biker had no injuries, they turned their attention to Kit who still protested he was fine. A gentle examination of the left-hand side of his body convinced the paramedic that he wasn't, especially as pulling his shirt up had revealed deep bruising rapidly developing down that same side.

'I'm sorry sir, we're going to have to insist you come with us. There may be internal bleeding. Not all injuries are apparent.'

Eventually realising they were right but still muttering curses under his breath, he limped over to the ambulance with them.

'Told you so' smiled Marje, 'Good luck.'

'I'm going with him, seeing as it's my fault' said Annie, her bottom lip still trembling.

'Oh Annie, let's not go through that again. It was no-one's fault, it was an accident, pure and simple. And you can't come with me. I need you to go and check on the dogs for me. Here's the key.'

As he sat on the ambulance steps and pulled the key out, Annie said,

'My hero!' She made it sound like a joke but he really was. He hadn't thought twice about putting her dog's safety before his own.

Chess, who hadn't left Annie's side having learnt her lesson the hard way, now put her paws on the step below and reached up to give Kit's cheek two wet and sloppy licks.

'Look, you're her hero too' smiled Annie. 'You saved Chess. She wouldn't have survived that blow' and embarrassingly, she started crying again.

'I couldn't let anything happen to her could I? Stop worrying, I'll be back in a couple of hours.'

The ambulance driver cleared his throat apologetically.

'They'll be wanting to keep you in overnight I'm afraid sir, for tests. Will you be able to look after his dogs a bit longer?' He turned to Annie.

'Oh for Chri…' began Kit.

Annie interrupted him. 'Of course I will. Just do as you're told Kit. Please?'

Kit raised his eyes to heaven but turned round slowly to climb into the ambulance, flinching as he did so.

The ambulance set off and the crowd went back to their lives with plenty gossip to keep them going for a week, while Annie made her tearful way up to Hunter's Lodge, both woman and dog keeping each other very close.

Chapter 26

Apart from nipping back to her cottage with the dogs to explain to her neighbours and shove a few things into a bag, Annie had spent the rest of the day up at Kit's. As often happens, at first she wasn't too worried about Kit but as the day progressed and she had too much time to think, she imagined that there *had* been internal bleeding and maybe he'd have to be operated on to stop it.

She paced up and down the floors of the Lodge. She washed his breakfast pots up, thinking at the same time that he must have got back late last night. She scoured the library shelves for a humorous book to cheer her up when it came to bed-time. She set up the settee with cushions and the throw off the back, she didn't want to go wandering around upstairs, it seemed wrong somehow. She had rung the hospital but they didn't tell her anything apart from he was comfortable, as she wasn't a relative.

Finally, she let the dogs out of the front door and set off towards the Winterfell Stone with them all. She needed this to walk off the anxiety, although the dogs would never complain about going on their favourite walk either. She bombed along the path with her head down, looking neither right nor left.

Whatever Kit said, she felt responsible. She mustn't have been holding Chess's lead firmly enough, although she would never have imagined she would pull away from her like that. She normally stuck by her side, no matter what. The thing is, Chess loved Kit almost as much as she loved Annie. She tried not to think of the jumble of feelings she was experiencing about Kit. Best to ignore them.

The Stone appeared to her right but she didn't stop. She continued up until she reached the far edge of the wood. There was an overgrown path that carried on to another large area of woodland over to the left. She negotiated this path behind the dogs and saw that it formed a boundary between the two areas of land. To her right, the land rose gradually revealing beyond the rough grazing and drystone walls, the purple-coloured fells, shadows dancing across them changing their contours.

To her left, the field had sheep grazing in it so Annie immediately put the dogs on their leads. Below the field of sheep were what looked like extensive grounds behind which a large house stood sentinel over the rural scene around it. She realised she was looking at the back of Huntingdon Hall. This was perhaps the path that Kit had mentioned before, overgrown but leading from the Hall. It could be used again with only a little work if the plans for the Stone site ever came to fruition.

Thinking about Kit made her realise she ought to get back in case he rang. The sun had lost its strength and was sending watery shapes across the countryside. Letting the dogs off the lead again near to the Stone, she was struck again by the feelings it produced. Whether it was because her emotions were all over the place , a strong impulse now radiated in her brain. The compulsion took over – she just *had* to touch the Stone.

Telling the dogs to 'Sit – Stay' like a latter-day Barbara Woodhouse, she left them there and made her way quickly to the Stone, fairly secure that the

'Evil Farmer' wouldn't be around at this late stage in the day.

Taking a quick look around, she leant forward and put both hands on the Stone and closed her eyes. How many people over the centuries had felt the need to touch this stone and many more like them across Britain and the world. It was like a primeval instinct, a force coming from inside you, connecting the past with the present. There was no doubt that these ancient stones spoke to something inside the human breast, something we didn't understand ourselves. The ancient people were probably closer to understanding it than we are, she thought.

Annie concentrated hard and tried to feel the history and the lives of the people from countless generations ago. To bring the age-old community of Winterfell into her mind. Instead, she could only see Kit's face, his brown eyes changing colour in the evening light, his untamed hair flopping across one eyebrow, his mouth turning sensuously up at the corners as he smiled at her…

Her eyes shot open and she sprung back from the stone as if she had touched fire. It was so real! She turned slowly back to the path. It was almost as though he was there and she was leaving him behind. He just wouldn't leave her mind.

The three dogs, although sitting like coiled springs ready to jump up at a moment's notice, were still exactly where she had left them. She never ceased to be amazed at how intelligent sheepdogs were. Bred over the years to be man's working companion, they were alert to every change in their owner's attitude and showed the utmost loyalty to them. As she reached them, she made a big fuss of them and gave them all one of the small treats she kept in her pocket. Time to go home, she whispered to them.

*

The dogs went straight to their water bowls as Annie put the kettle on but then stood at the glass door leading out to the side of the house, whimpering and whining.

'You've just been out for over an hour and you want to go out again?' she admonished.

They looked back at her with strange little snuffling noises at the bottom of the door. Annie began to get worried. While not quite isolated here, she couldn't bang on the walls for help like she could at the cottage. Not that she'd ever needed to. Another thought took over – could it be Gardman?

She walked over, in two minds. One mind said 'Make sure the door is locked and bolted' and the other mind said 'Surely they would be barking viciously if they felt threatened?' A third mind joined in the thinking, 'Maybe if I let them out and it's an intruder they'll bite him and scare him off?'.

The third mind won and she opened the door to let them out and at the same time, grabbing a knife from the draining board next to the door. As the dogs ran out, the whimpering turned to yelps of joy as they stopped a little further down the verandah, making a fuss of the man who had just stepped onto it.

'Kit!' she shouted, as glad to see him as the dogs obviously were but annoyed at the same time. He mumbled something about a taxi dropping him off and waiting for her to get back as he hadn't got a key.

'You scared the life out of me. You're supposed to be in hospital till tomorrow. You nearly got this stuck in your chest to add to your other injuries.'

'I've discharged myself. They've done all the tests so…' he began then stopped.

Kit looked down at her hands then up at her again, his eyes crinkling.

'What were you going to do, whisk me to death?' he asked, then burst out laughing. 'Ouch, don't make me laugh'

He doubled over, half laughing, half wincing in pain as Annie looked down at the whisk in her hand, then back at the knife still lying on the draining board. Kit straightened up.

'Killing me by sledge and motorbike didn't work so you were going to try stabbing me? Painfully - with a whisk?'

He set off laughing again which made him double up in pain. Serves you right, thought Annie. She paused.

'So you do think it was my fault today then?' she didn't feel like joining in the laughter as his words sunk in.

'Oh Annie, you are too sensitive. It was a joke and I've already said it was an accident. Definition – an unfortunate incident that happens unintentionally and unexpectedly, typically resulting in injury - ! You could blame the motorcyclist for pulling out of the lane two minutes late, or Chess for pulling out of your hand because you weren't holding it in a grip of iron, or me for standing at the other side of the road in full view of Chess – or the planets aligning wrongly with the stars. The fact remains, it *was* an accident and if I ever hear you mention it again, you are barred from my house, the Stone Circle group, the pub and from Betty's in Harrogate. Now for heaven's sake, get the whisky out of that cupboard, I need something to numb the pain.

Grabbing the whisky from the cupboard he'd indicated; she found a glass. No, two as she needed to numb the pain of this strange day too. She headed outside again to find Kit. This side of the house, faced West, the same as the back of Meadow Cottage and caught the evening sun too. It was on its way down below the horizon now and soon it would be dark.

There was a long covered verandah , spanning this side of the Lodge. It had white columns supporting a small sloping roof and there were white painted railings along the outer edge with a gap for the two steps which led onto the grass. It was the kind you see in the American movies with an old lady with glasses on and white hair in a bun, knitting in a rocking chair.

Kit was sitting at one end on a chair next to a small wrought iron table, so she put the bottle and glasses down on the table and sat on the chair at the other side. She turned to him.

'Where are the rocking chairs with the crocheted covers?' she smiled sweetly.

'And the banjos?' he shot back.

They grinned at each other and at the same time, started humming the 'Duelling Banjos' tune from the Deliverance movie, breaking off after the first bar to laugh at their identical train of thought.

'Great minds…' she said.

Chapter 27

Kit, with the whisky glass in his hand, stretched his arm out to indicate a point in the distance, more or less straight ahead.

'Can you see the Winterfell Stone? The top of it?'

The mention of the Stone jolted Annie's memory. She must have just looked confused to Kit as he started to explain.

'With the Stone being on a plateau on top of the hill, you can see it from here during the day sometimes with binoculars, If the light is right. At least the top part of it.' He laughed at her expression. 'From the edge of my orchard at the back of the Lodge, you can see it even better as the land rises up there gradually towards Brytherstone. The best place to see it though, is from my bedroom upstairs. Would you like to have a look?'

Kit did the wiggling eyebrows and the twirling of a pretend moustache that morphed him into a pantomime villain.

'Why, Mr Courtney sir, I do believe you're flirting with me. Kindly desist. I ain't that sorta gal!' she laughed, and although she wouldn't have minded the flirting carrying on, joke or not, she had to tell him the news she had just been reminded of. Today's events had thrown it firmly to the back of her mind.

'So' she began 'the Stone is on land directly opposite this house?'

'If by opposite, you mean half a mile away as the crow flies, then yes it is.'

'Did you ever wonder why, if the Stone was once on Huntingdon Hall land as your Lodge was, why your boundary does a dog-leg detour at the end of your garden, follows the path around the wood and carries on past the hall? Wouldn't it have been easier for your forbears to have included the land with the Stone on when the land was divided into Hunter's Lodge land and Huntingdon Hall land? From the Lodge, up to the land the Stone is on, then back down to past the hall would make a perfect square. And perfect sense too.'

Kit looked across at her, suddenly serious and then pushed himself up to go back into the kitchen. Annie sat still, hardly daring to breathe. Had she upset him? It was a sensitive subject and she shouldn't have made it like an interrogation. However, he came back out with some matches and lit two large candles placed on an old metal flower trough under the railings in front of them. The flames flickered into life and he turned to her, the light dancing on his face. Playing on his cheekbones. Reflecting in his eyes.

'It would have made perfect sense, I agree. Unfortunately, the Land Registry and Ordnance Survey maps show this is not the case and are evidence that the most sensible and practical course is sometimes not taken.'

'And the maps show that the land the Winterfell Stone is on, belong to Farmer Gardman and his forebears?'

The Land registry shows his grandfather registered it but before that, the records have been lost. However, in the absence of other evidence, it has to be taken as true, There is no reason to doubt it according to officials, although I did – and still do. I'm like you and can't understand why the land would veer off like it does-and why a farmer would purchase it from the Hall when it's not even good farming land. I have argued this point so many times and have gone round in so many circles that I am in danger of disappearing up my own backside.'

Annie persisted. 'Have you got any old maps? Is that where they get the ordnance survey maps from?'

'When the O.S.maps started in the early 19th century, the land was already designated to the farm. The then owner showed evidence he had farmed that same land for many years before. So the O.S. just surveyed the land they were told belonged to the farmer. There is no evidence – and I have checked and double checked the evidence from the old books up at the Hall - that the land belongs to that farm but none that it belongs to the Hall either. The deeds are very old and don't show the further reaches of land in detail and there were a lot of private conveyances which is what could have happened with Gardman's farm, which was once one of the Hall's tenant farms in the 17th century. The Hall sold off a lot of the tenant farm land and houses in the 19th century. All the other deeds have been found with evidence of this but not for that parcel of land as that original farm didn't have the Stone on its land. It was always on Courtney land before with no proof apart from occasional mentions in the dusty tomes at the Hall but no proof positive. It could also be unregistered land, in which case Gardman has the upper hand as his family registered it with the land registry many years ago as I explained.

I'm sorry, I sound like I'm lecturing you on the long sorry process you have to go through to prove ownership of land. I don't know why but to me, the Land Registry seem to be favouring Gardman but I think that's just a touch of neurosis on my part. You can see why I have been so frustrated. The truth of the matter is, that without proof telling us otherwise, the land belongs to Gardman.'

Annie felt a mounting sense of excitement.

'You looked through all the old books at the Hall?'

'Yes, everything that still remained after the fire in the library in the mid-nineteenth century anyway. Most of the books and archives were saved by the staff. Why the Spanish Inquisition, Senorita Millford?' he smiled, alert to the fact that there was something behind the questions.

'Would Wentforth's father or grandfather have sold any land since your grandfather sold it to them?' she continued, ignoring his question.

'Not a chance. Gardman's family was always causing trouble in those days too and Alfred remembers how annoyed his father was at not retaining some of the farms in the first place because he could have used them for branches of his family. Annie? What's all this about?'

Kit stared straight at her, holding her gaze even though she was almost jumping up and down on her seat. In answer to his question, she dashed into the kitchen to fetch her phone. Kneeling down next to him, she found the photos she had taken of the map in the old book and handed it to him. She saw his brows knit together as he bent over and brought the magnification up. Then she saw his mouth drop open. He had seen the same thing she had when she'd looked at the map. The land went down from the far edge of Kit's orchard behind the lodge, then over to the west in a straight line across the land, encompassing the land where the Stone now stood. If this could be construed as proof, the Stone was on Kit's land!

After a full two minutes of staring at it without taking his eyes off the screen he asked,

'Where did you find this?'

'The library'

'The *library*?'

'In a huge leather book in a cupboard with a load of other books that haven't been looked at in years, according to Min'

'The library' he repeated incredulously.

'It's a really old book' she went on 'dating to 1783, a hundred years after the present Hall was built. And if there is no proof that the land hasn't been sold to Gardman's family, then I would say, with this, you have got at least an equal chance of success – and more clout behind your claims.'

'I have no idea why it was in the library. Perhaps it was lent to them or maybe taken to the library after the fire for safekeeping as it had just opened then? Whatever the reason, I'm just so glad you've found it because this map, in the absence of any other but the O.S. one afterwards, should still stand!'

Kit flung himself from the chair, then clutched his side, belatedly remembering the bruising.

'Come on' he said, grabbing Annie's hand.

'Where are we going?' she asked.

'The library of course.'

'What? Are you crazy? It's night-time and besides, I haven't got the keys.'

'But – this could be my land – and if it isn't mine, it's Alfred's and he'll at least let us dig there.'

268

'If it is your land, it will still be your land in the morning. We'll go there first thing, I promise you. Now – bed!'

Immediately the word was out of her mouth, she felt her cheeks reddening, although in his present state, he probably hadn't registered it.

He had.

'Why, Miss Millford' he replied in an even worse version of her earlier deep South accent 'I had no idea you were such a forward young lady.'

She ignored him, even though her cheeks were shining like beacons now.

'You need sleep. You've got a lot of detective work to do tomorrow and you need to rest mind and body before that. Upstairs.'

She pointed to the stairs and he said,

'Are you going home then?'

'No' she said, indicating the settee. 'I'm sleeping there as you never know with injuries like yours. I'd rather be here on hand. You might need me in the middle of the night.'

Oh god. Mouth open – foot right in. What was wrong with her? She saw the wide grin appearing on Kit's face. It suddenly disappeared and a gentle expression came into his eyes. He stepped towards her, put his hand behind her head and brought his face to his, dropping the lightest of kisses on her lips but lingering a second too long. He pulled away.

'Thank you Annie. For everything.' Then he went upstairs. It took Annie hours to get to sleep and it was nothing to do with how comfortable the settee was.

Diary

The last May Day committee meeting is tomorrow. I'm not sure I'm ready for this but there's no going back now. Nobody knows about it. No one except Percy. I just had to use someone as a sounding board. I was going to talk it over with Annie but she had a bit of a shock with her dog and Kit in an accident. They were together yesterday, asking if they could look at an old book from the cupboard. I couldn't see why not as it belonged to the Courtney family in the first place by the look of it. They took a few photos, asked me to keep it under lock and key and let nobody near it, then Kit dashed off urgently. Annie is moving up to the Lodge to look after all the dogs for a few days, so it must be important. I didn't feel like I could trouble her as she has enough on.

So instead, I took the plunge and invited Percy over for dinner. I've never invited anyone to eat here before or anywhere for that matter, so I felt nervous for that reason too as well as the main reason.

It was only pork chops, mashed potato and veg. I'm a plain cook and no culinary genius but he seemed to like it. When I started apologising, he stopped me and said he much preferred plain meals.

That boosted my confidence a little , enough to push a couple of sheets of paper under his nose when we were having coffee.

He smiled and read them slowly before turning to me with an uncharacteristically serious expression on his face. I've done the wrong thing, I thought. He won't want anything more to do with me after this. Tears sprang to my eyes. I hadn't realised how much his approval meant to me until now.

Before I could blink the tears away, he took hold of both my hands and looked me straight in the eye, something neither of us do very often.

'Am I to understand that you are going to read this out at the meeting tomorrow?' Oh heavens, he looked quite horrified and so was I when I realised tears were falling down my cheeks and I couldn't stop them. I nodded.

'Minerva, I'm not sure why you feel the need to do this as I'm sure no one is against you in the slightest. Apart from Mr Gardman of course - and he's against everyone in general.'

He gave a little smile and I tried to smile back. He looked down at the papers again.

'You have written so eloquently and persuasively that if anyone IS against you, which I seriously doubt, then your words will convince them otherwise. I have always had nothing but respect ...' he glanced down briefly and continued in a gentler voice '...and more, for you and I will be there at the meeting to support you, one hundred percent on your side, as I always have been.'

At this, I embarrassed myself further by doing a peculiar sort of hiccup and started sobbing. Loudly. So very unlike me. What is happening to me?

Dear Percy, he went to the sideboard and poured us a brandy from a bottle I've had since Christmas and slowly, we fell back into easy conversation again. Before he went he wished me luck and told me to save him a place on the front row. Then he turned round at the door and said 'Maybe it would help me get over the worry it's caused me by agreeing to have lunch with him at the pub on Sunday?'

'Is this a date?' I smiled, far too flirty for a staid matron of my age and my cheeks were SO red when I realised what I'd said.

'It certainly is, my dear' he smiled and suddenly, I knew that tomorrow's speech wouldn't be such an ordeal after all, knowing he was there for me - and that he believed in me. This feels like a dream. Can you fall in love in your inert middle -age? It really feels like it. I am going to close this diary now and go to bed and hope I wake up in less of a teenage frame of mind.

(read loudly and confidently!)

"Forgive me for hijacking your May Day meeting but after the rumours of recent weeks, I would like to dispel a few myths and tell you what Druids today stand for. Druids are made up of teachers, doctors, dustmen, writers, cricketers, writers, lawyers – and even librarians… It doesn't change us as a person, we are still the same people you have always known.

We are ecologically conscious and as committed to the environment and every living thing as we can be. We promote environmental causes such as tree planting in a peaceful way as Nature is at the root of our belief system. We promote harmony and connection with the Natural world and the elements of sky, earth, water, wind, stone, sun, moon and stars.

When you think we are 'contacting spirits', well perhaps we are. As we believe that every living thing has a spirit; a soul. Even stones are imbued with a spirit of the past. They are sentinels amongst, as much as trees are and have been there long before man came on this Earth.

Yet contacting spirits, for me personally, means remembering our ancestors and our own families through the generations. Remembering and respecting all the communities that lived in houses on this land around us here. In Winterfell.

I stand for peace and giving back to Nature. I trained as a minister of the Church of England and I am a Christian as well as a Druid. The two, contrary to popular belief, are not mutually incompatible.

I am passionate about the village. You may think I am a relative newcomer but my family have lived here in this very village for many generations. Since at least the fifteen hundreds when there was first mention of a Pryde in the church records. That is my family name, through my mother and grandmother. You will see the name on gravestones at the church

My grandmother, some of you might remember was Dulcie Pryde, and lived where I now live? She kept her maiden name and I'm thinking of changing mine to the old family name too, as my family have been Guardians of the Winterfell Stone for hundreds of years. It is a role I have taken on gladly. As Guardian, I ask for peace, health and happiness for our community and ask for the spirit of Nature to bless us all, when I visit the Stone.

You may not think it works but it doesn't do any harm either. And neither do I — and so I simply ask for your tolerance

and for your understanding. Thank
you."

Midsummer

(Known as *'Litha'* – Bede.)

The old Summer began on May 1st *(Beltane)* and ended on August 1st *(Lammas)* *Midsummer* was roughly halfway between.

Chapter 28

The May day committee – and half of the residents of Winterfell - had retired to the Hunter's Moon pub to dry out after the celebrations on the school field. The rain had started during the latter part but didn't seem to have sent anyone home or put anyone off the attractions.

Both the headmistress, Mrs Knight and Cynthia, the vicar, sat at a large round table in the corner, their 'drowned rat' appearance having nothing to do with the rain. Cynthia didn't wear make-up but Mrs. Knight had rivulets of mascara dried onto her cheeks. Annie pointed it out in case she wanted to remove it.

'It was supposed to be waterproof mascara!' she complained 'but I am too exhausted now to bother. I will wear my battle scars with pride. I have to say Cynthia that it was good of you to volunteer in Mr Mountford's place when he couldn't make it. '

'I enjoyed it, if you can call having soaking wet sponges hitting you in the face at 30 miles per hour, enjoyment' she laughed 'but I must admit that I thought the children would mostly aim for you and not me!'

'It was your baptism of fire – or water' smiled Maisie, who had been persuaded to come along with Annie, 'It's probably a test by the non-churchgoers to see what a good sport you are. I think you've definitely proved it to them today.'

The headmistress stood up and went to have a quick word with Trevor who was enjoying all the trade being brought in. Turning round, she addressed the pub, her voice carrying so well, it took you back to school assemblies.

'I would just like to take this opportunity, as so many of you are gathered here, to thank you all for your input today. Whether it was helping on the stalls, organising, clearing up in the rain, or just attending and helping to swell the funds for St Martin's hospice. You have all stayed cheerful, despite the weather and it has been a huge success.

The school field is only small and you filled it but hopefully next year, we may be able to hold it up at the Winterfell Stone if we get permission, and have an even bigger celebration. Although I'm so exhausted after this that I'm having second thoughts'

Mrs Knight laughed then became serious.

'This village has a great community spirit and is a wonderful place to bring your children up. You all pull together when something needs doing. We couldn't have done it without you.' The whole pub was silent, listening to her words. 'So give yourself a big round of applause!'

A big cheer went up around the room and from through in the tap room at the other side of the bar. Applause echoed round the pub. I LOVE this village, thought Annie. Then she noticed Kit had come through the main door and was standing there, looking very serious. He had been away, trying to reclaim his land and from the couple of 'texts of few words' she had received, it was proving tricky. He had engaged a lawyer and was prepared to take it to court. He had missed the May Day celebrations too; he must have just got back. Annie just wanted to put her arms round him and hug him, he looked so tired. She watched him as he slowly went up to the headmistress and took her place when she came over to sit back down.

'If I can just keep you a minute longer' began Kit in a voice used to lecture halls, 'I have some news regarding the land Mrs Knight mentioned. The land around our Stone.

As many of you know, I have been fighting to get Gardman to let us use the land, both for archaeological purposes and for village community occasions, as the field has plenty space without having to disturb the possible stone circle. What most of you don't know is that, because of the detective work by our own Annie Millford,' he indicated over to where she sat and many pairs of eyes followed. Annie was bright red and took a gulp of her wine. 'from something she found at the library, it shows I have a valid claim on the land.

I have been chasing up the legalities of this but have been thwarted at every turn by Gardman who puts obstacles in the way constantly. Until, that is, that I threatened to get a lawyer to fight him through the courts and sue him. This hit him where it would hurt, in his wallet. His solicitor finally admitted his claim is a tenuous one and as we had produced new evidence, his client didn't want to lose money going to court. Gardman only had one stipulation, just to save face a little, and that was that he could graze his sheep on my lands – and they *are* Hunter's Lodge lands. I was quite happy to comply with that as it saves me cutting the grass myself! So – the land is mine – but it is also ours. It belongs to the village along with the Stone. So all being well, Mrs Knight, you *will* be holding your next May Day up there!'

There was another great roar, louder than the first and Kit disappeared into a crowd all trying to slap him on the back, ask for details and to buy him a pint. Trevor pre-empted this by handing one over to him and he drank half of it in one go, which produced another cheer. Eventually, he came across to the table where Percy had moved them all around to make room for another chair. Kit smiled at Annie as he sat down and raised his glass 'To Annie' he said quietly and as all her friends raised their glasses to her.

'A wonderful joint effort, I would say' said Min ' and I am going to be very cheeky now'

'Steady on Minerva' smiled Percy and she dug him in the ribs.

'The Summer solstice is coming up next month, is there any chance at all that the village can celebrate it up there? I will be there of course, with your permission, but it would be wonderful to share the occasion with everyone.'

Kit lay back against the chair and was quiet for a few seconds while the others held their breath.

'I have rung the archaeological team I am in charge of, who are up in Scotland, and we are going to make a start straight away on the buried stones as we have wasted so much time …'

He looked at the silent group around the table, all waiting for his next words and looking rather deflated.

'…but we can start at the far side and fence it off to make it safe for everyone. So, subject to a lot of organisation – I mean a *lot* – I would be happy to make Midsummer the first celebration at the Winterfell Stone.'

There was another cheer from all at the table. Anyone listening outside to all the whoops, roars and clapping of the evening would be forgiven for thinking a WWF wrestling match was going on inside.

'I'm sorry to miss the May Day event – and the last committee meeting. How did it go?' asked Kit, looking directly at Min. Annie had mentioned a speech Min had given to the committee in a text.

'It went really well' Percy answered for her. 'Everyone was really interested in the Druid aspect and they wanted to find out more. There weren't any new recruits though, were there?'

Percy smiled at Min and it touched Annie's heart. Somehow in the past few days, things had changed between these two, for the better.

'It went very well and I feel very encouraged now. There was only one sour note wasn't there? Your friend, Mrs Whitehouse'

'She's not my friend' objected Percy until he realised she was teasing.

'She still tried to voice her biases but was shot down by Maisie.'

'By Maisie?' repeated Kit in astonishment.

'She was like a little tiger' laughed Annie 'Telling this harridan that her husband studied, wrote about and approved of the modern-day Druids and their link to Nature and so did she. And "hadn't she realised she was in a minority of one!" At which point Mrs Whitehouse looked around her, stuck her nose up in the air and walked out to a whispered 'Good riddance' from some of the crowd.'

Maisie looked fierce again.

'Silly woman, she was only complaining as she'd had her nose put out of joint – Percy was paying far more attention to Minerva than to her.'

This was so un-Maisie-like, that a howl of laughter went round the table, with Maisie joining in.

'So' continued Kit when they had quietened down. 'Who is going to organise it? Could it perhaps be the Stone Circle group, many of who are here tonight? That way you could liaise with me regarding the Dig and I will keep any works well away from public areas. What do you think?'

Everyone thought it was a good idea and the rest of the evening was spent trying ideas out with each other. A few of them volunteered for various roles and by general consensus, as Kit would be otherwise engaged most of the time, Annie and Min were appointed chief organisers.

Annie walked home with Kit to collect Chess from the Lodge where she had left all three dogs after the afternoon's entertainment. She left him to sleep as he didn't look like he'd slept in weeks. Explanations of his battle could come later. Before she stepped onto the path, he dropped a gentle kiss on her cheek and stroked her hair before Chess pulled her towards home.

Chapter 29

Afternoon tea at Meadow Cottage was almost ready. It was a bright, sunny afternoon and everyone was sitting in Annie's garden at borrowed tables and chairs. They were set up at the bottom of the garden on the patio area to take advantage of the open views over the dale, although everyone seemed too preoccupied with chattering to each other rather than looking at the view. Annie supposed they had become blasé about their surroundings having lived here for so long but she thought she would never fail to appreciate the far-reaching scene that spread out from the back of her cottage. The warmth of the afternoon had the men stripped down to their shirts and the women in sleeveless tops, apart from Maisie and Ada who sported smart tea-dresses.

The kitchen table was groaning with neat sandwiches of egg and cress, ham and smoked salmon and cream cheese, cut into triangles with the crusts cut off. There were scones and cakes galore. Everyone was here now apart from Min, who had just phoned to say she was on her way. Kit couldn't be there as he was busy organising and tidying up the dig so it could be finished temporarily for this week. Tomorrow they would need to start setting up the land for the Midsummer festival at the weekend.

Ada was busying herself collecting knives and spoons for the jam and cream to take out. As she exited the back door, Maisie entered, asking if she could do anything.

'I think I've got everything under control thanks Maisie. Maybe take the serviettes out? They're in that cupboard.'

Gavin poked his head in the back door.

'Can I help?'

'No, it's okay thanks. Oh, hang on, can you take the plates out now please? Just put them on the long table and everyone can take one.'

The main core of the Stone Circle group were waiting outside and Min would be here any minute. Annie went to her front window to look for her before she put any food on the tables.

Opposite, she could see Cynthia at the church lych-gate, talking to a tall, thin man in a suit. The vicar had said she had an appointment but would look in later, so to make sure they saved her some food. Her appetite was legendary. Annie turned her head to look down the lane. There was no sign of Min but as she went to turn away, she caught sight of a dark-haired woman embracing a man, who was now kissing her warmly on the cheek before giving her a hug. It hardly registered at first but when it did, Annie felt herself going hot and cold and she gripped the windowsill. Kit! Kissing Isolde! That was more than a kiss of greeting – and Kit wasn't a natural hugger or in the habit of bestowing kisses on people. And there had been history between them years before. Had it been rekindled?

Annie's mouth felt dry and she swallowed hard as she turned away. She felt utterly betrayed.

Why? She tried to apply logic to the situation. She and Kit were only friends and there had only been tentative gestures between them that might have made her think otherwise. Neither she nor Kit had ever made a hazy situation clear. Perhaps they were too frightened to but the fact remained that Kit had a perfect right to kiss any woman he wanted. Except Isolde. Annie glowered at the thought. They had history that had somehow just now merged with the present. All that about her chasing Kit – no one was making him kiss her *that* fondly!

Annie sniffed and realised how ridiculously near to tears she was. Annoyed with herself, she pulled herself together and stomped into the kitchen. Marje had joined Maisie and Ada in the kitchen and was getting some beer she'd brought with her, out of the fridge. There was a silent and expectant pause and Annie only realised how thunderous her expression must be when she looked up and saw all three of them staring at her with puzzled expressions.

'We'll start to take the food out. Min will be here anytime now' she snapped.

Nobody moved. Just then there was a knock and the front door opened.

'Sorry I'm late' Min shouted through 'Mm, that all looks good'

Min came through and was eyeing the heavily laden kitchen table.

'It certainly does' came a voice from behind her. Annie whipped her head round to see Kit standing there, his hand reaching towards a platter 'Can I pinch a couple of these sandwiches?'

'No!' screeched Annie, slapping his hand away. 'I've only made enough for the people who said they'd be here.'

There was another long pause in which Kit withdrew his hand, looking like a puppy who'd been kicked – and the women looked down at the mountain of sandwiches, then at each other, then finally at Annie, in one smooth action.

Annie felt her cheeks burning and picked up a tray of glasses, then put it down again, took a large gulp of the wine she'd poured herself earlier, then picked the tray up again.

'I'm sorry, yes, I can see that you might, yes...' Kit stuttered, looking totally confused. 'I'll just slink off back to the dig then? Without a sandwich?'

'Fine' spat Annie, taking the tray out, aware of the raised eyebrows behind her, whether she could see them or not. By the time she stomped her way back into the kitchen, there was just Min and Maisie left there, huddled together, the latter of whom made a hasty exit into the garden. Min pointed to the enormous platter of sandwiches.

'I'll just take these meagre portions out to the starving masses then shall I?'

Annie eyed her uncertainly as Min stepped towards her.

'I can guess why you're not your usual sunny self. I know what you think you saw earlier because I was a few yards behind Kit, trying to catch him up-but you're wrong. He'd been to the hardware shop for a sledgehammer to replace a broken one. They're fencing off the far side of the dig from the land we're using for the festival.

Isolde and her fiancé were booking their wedding with the vicar at the church. Isolde turned and saw Kit who looked like a rabbit caught in the headlights until she announced the imminent marriage. I get the feeling she thought it would make him jealous but her couldn't hide his delight that she'd finally given up on him.'

Annie looked abashed and her shoulders slumped back from their earlier position of around her ears. Then she recovered herself quickly.

'Not that it matters to me. I just hoped he wasn't getting involved with another man's woman.' She said shiftily, not daring to look at Min in the eye. When she did, she found Min was looking at her with an amused but kind expression.

'Don't you think it's about time you admitted you have feelings for Kit. That you like him – a lot. And not just as a friend. When you relax enough to admit this and stop ignoring it because you think you'll get hurt or you've convinced yourself you don't want love, I think you'll find that he feels exactly the same. I know this from experience and from someone who once, very tactfully, gave me the benefit of her wisdom.'

Annie was going to protest but realised it was no use. Min was right, after all.

'So...the student becomes the Master?' she said.

They grinned at each other before Marje clattered in to put the kettle on.

*

When Annie had stopped doing her Incredible Sulk impressions, she settled down to enjoy a pleasant afternoon. As usual, with these special people, the conversation flowed, as did the tea out of the teapots dotted on the tables. The sun shone down on them and everything looked like one of those mellow 50s films with a dreamy, hazy quality to the light. Chess was in her element, going from table to table with imploring eyes, daring people not to think how cute she was. Of course they all thought she was.

She was asked if she didn't feel like staying on here after her year was up – they'd be sad to see her go, they said. She smiled and let them know that she had already rung the agent up. The Prestons had decided to stay in Australia, so the cottage was hers to rent for another year, with an option to buy at the end. This announcement produced a gratifying reaction, especially from her three neighbours.

Everyone put the finishing details to their roles on the Saturday evening and slowly drifted away. Annie refused their offers of clearing up but everyone mucked in and it was done in no time. Maisie was the last to leave and she opened the fridge, reaching in to the back, bringing out a container.

'I put a few sandwiches aside and wrapped some carrot cake up in foil.'

Annie looked at her, puzzled.

'For Kit. I thought you might want to give the poor starving lad some food?' she laughed. 'He'll just be finishing up now if you want to nip up there?'

Ah, *Two* matchmakers, thought Annie.

They walked out of the cottage together, Annie turning to look at the roses growing round her door. She remembered wondering what it would look like when she arrived in the depths of winter. Now she knew. It was glorious and the smell just made her want to linger. Not too long though as she was on a mission to humiliate herself. She wondered if he was angry with her?

There was no answer at the Lodge and no dogs barking either and Chess was looking eagerly up the pathway, so she carried on up to the Stone.

The others were clearing away and she waved at a couple of the girls she had spoken to in the pub. Kit was still bent over examining something and didn't even look up when Bella and Bessie ran full pelt towards Chess with a loud doggie greeting. She walked over to him.

'I've er, brought you some sandwiches, there were some left over'

He looked up at her and smiled with that lovely, twinkly, gentle look in his eyes.

'I bid a hasty retreat but I'm glad you've saved me something – I haven't eaten since breakfast.'

Annie felt even worse now.

'I'm really sorry about earlier, I was in a bit of a mood'

'I noticed. Not like you, apart from when you're confronted by angry farmers. Alright now?'

Well, if he knew what her mood was about, he was keeping quiet about it, thank goodness.

'I'm fine. How is it coming along?' she waved at the general area round the dig.

'Really exciting! What we've discovered in the last few days is that this part…' and he indicated a straight line from the direction she had come in, up to the Stone 'may have been a processional way. A ceremonial entrance to the stone circle and the Stone itself. The people would have come up through the village and then turned left to walk towards the sun, or the sun setting over the Stone perhaps. Near to the circle, we're pretty sure it's a circle now, there are a few stone fragments in place which would have formed a path up to the stone and there is evidence of post holes going further back for about fifty yards.' He pointed in the direction of the Lodge. 'So yes, very excited.'

His face was open, eager and happy. She beamed at him and went forward to embrace him.

'It's well overdue' she whispered to him.

'What, the discovery or the hug?' he winked, only half-joking. She blushed and turned back towards home.

'Enjoy your sandwiches' she shouted back.

'See you on Saturday' he shouted with a smile before tucking into the sandwiches like a ravenous wolf.

Midsummer

'But all the story of the night told over,
    And all their minds transfigur'd so together,
    More witnesseth than fancy's images
    And grows to something of great constancy...'
Hippolyta. Act 5, Scene 1.
    A Midsummer Night's Dream – Shakespeare.

*

'There is an ancient oral tradition in the village and surroundings of Winterfell in North Yorkshire. It concerns the Winterfell Stone, an ancient monument rising above the village. Legend has it that if any young person touches the stone at Midsummer, they will dream of their future spouse
'History of the Craven district of North Yorkshire'
- Prof. Theodore Brown.

*

Min looked around her at the people laughing, drinking, dancing and generally enjoying themselves. Children were shrieking with joy and dogs were joining in with excited yaps. There was music playing- a traditional Irish folk band that Kit knew from his student days – and people were reacting to the tunes in the age-old way. They let themselves go, Their inhibitions about what they looked like or their standing in the community was gone. They were just having the time of their lives. A curly-haired young boy with the band sang an old song in an ancient language. People stopped dancing for a while to listen to his beautiful voice.

The bonfire had been lit at the far right and was being patrolled by Frank and Aidan who were in their element, being closet pyromaniacs. What was it with men and fire? Probably that was primeval too, right from the first very important discovery that the sun wasn't the only source of warmth and light.

There were fire pits dotted about to give light and heat in a more manageable manner and Kit and some of his team had put a pathway of torches ready to light at either side of the newly discovered processional way. They led right up to and under the Stone itself. The air was still warm. The sun was a burnt orange semi-circle now. It was time.

*

Annie helped herself to the food and just in time too, She never thought the feast the villagers had provided would even have a dent made in it but there was something about being outside in the fresh air, even if it was getting dark now. There was something about laughter and dancing. Everyone had voracious appetites and the food was fast disappearing.

There had been enormous quantities of pork and chicken from the butchers and huge whole salmons donated by Alfred Wentforth and cooked by their chef. There was a variety of vegetables, both cooked or raw with dips, from Tom and his friends from the allotment association in the village. Tom had helped provide some of the new potatoes that were a traditional midsummer dish too. Nothing tasted better than new potatoes pulled out of the ground less than ten hours ago. They were served with soured cream and dill. Bright-coloured salads were dotted about the tables. Mouth-watering loaves of every type and shape had been laid out but were severely depleted now, as well as the cheddar and the wensleydale cheese that accompanied them.

Berries of different hues had been piled up in large bowls with cream from the creamery over at Brytherstone on the side. For those who didn't want the berries, and that wasn't many by the state of the bowls now, there was traditional honey cake, baked by Maisie, Ada, Cynthia and Frank and Aidan's wives in great batches.

An open-fronted beer tent had been set up by Marje and Trevor, selling hot mulled cider, mead and ales. They were doing a roaring trade. Like Trevor had said, nobody would go to the pub tonight anyway and this way, they could enjoy themselves too.

Annie found Marje, in front of the folk band and dancing wildly, declaring that the mead was 'a lot stronger than you think, so be careful' while obviously not following her own advice. Chess had joined with Bessie and Bella and half the dogs of the village and were alternating between having 'funny half-hours' chasing their tails and then looking pleadingly at people sat down at tables, eating. She would have to put Chess on a diet, starting tomorrow.

Frank and Aidan's wives had joined them over at the bonfire and were doing sedate little jigs and holding their summer dresses above their knees as though it was the time to rid yourself of any prudery. Cynthia was standing just behind her, in conversation with one of the archaeological team. They were discussing paganism, Christianity and the Romans – both ruddy-cheeked and talking nineteen to the dozen.

Tom, Ada and Maisie were all sitting round at a table from which emanated gales of laughter, although they kept casting furtive glances around as though they were fifteen-year- olds drinking in a pub.

Alfred and his family were sitting at another table. The family obviously now included Gavin who was clasping Wendy's hand like she might float off, while they stared into each other's eyes. None of them were dancing but their appearance was very welcome and they seemed to be having a good time. Even Isolde who Annie noticed had cracked her face into the approximation of a smile.

Kit. Where was Kit? An hour ago, he had taken a guitar offered by one of the band and had sung an Irish love song while looking straight at her. She hoped that wasn't in her imagination. She didn't think so. She'd seen him earlier telling Percy all about the processional way and post holes and ditches. Percy, to his credit, had looked very knowledgeable but had now disappeared. Suddenly she saw Kit, talking to one of the band who had now taken a break. The music was noticeable in its absence, music made the night seem more real. More magical. He suddenly turned towards her as though he knew exactly where she was. He smiled and kept smiling in her direction even though the musician was still rattling on regardless. His attention was distracted and he nodded across at someone. Percy, who was now standing next to Min. As though they had been waiting for his command, Kit nodded at some other men from the village and they stepped forward towards the torches in their stands. With one person to each of the torches, on Kit's signal, they lit them all. The drums started up, keeping a persistent rhythm. Kit was under the Winterfell Stone, lighting the very last one, which cast a spellbinding glow over the Stone, as though it was lit up from inside. It was time.

*

Minerva Jones walked between the avenue of burning torches up towards the Stone. The Stone she guarded and protected. It was in its proper place now, the focus of the community. Although the purpose may have changed from five thousand years ago, the people were still a community, still lived and toiled here. Were the same people in their hopes and dreams.

The sun was hanging over the top of the Stone now, making the Stone appear to project forward, silhouetted against the diminishing orange glow. Behind her, the villagers followed silently, headed by Kit, Annie and Cynthia. A little in front of the Stone she stopped. The sun was diffused, mesmerising. At that stage between dark and light, where the veil between the worlds is thinnest. She turned round to address the people. The time had come.

*

'Midsummer's Eve is the wedding of Heaven and Earth. It is when the battle of light and dark takes place. It is the longest day before we start our journey towards the winter days. We come to ask the blessing of the sun and the stone.'

She turned around and knelt before the stone, her arms held up towards the disappearing sun.

'Sacred earth, hold this stone firm. Let the spirit of our stone bless our village and keep it safe.

Peace of the earth and the sky to you. Blessings of the quiet moon and the stars to you. Peace and blessings to us all. Blessed be. '

*

Annie was moved to tears. There was a stunned but joyous silence after Min's words and then a cheer and then murmurs of 'Blessings to you' and 'Blessed be.' Even though many of them had no idea of the traditions, it just seemed fitting

305

tonight. It just seemed right and respectful. Most of them looked at the Stone in a new way, as they did with Min. They went up and shook her hand or hugged her. Percy hugged her too and to Annie's mind, this was what Min had been working towards all he life. She hoped she had found the happiness she deserved.

The lights from the firepits and the torches kicked in now it was darker and the band struck up their music once more. People moved away from the Stone and started their dancing again. Whirling, stomping, forming circles, they let themselves enjoy the night.

Young girls with garlands round their heads thought of the time tonight when they would put the flowers under their pillows and dream of young men who they hoped to marry.

A pair of hands squeezed Annie's shoulders and a lingering kiss was dropped onto the back of her neck. She turned to see Kit, his face in half shadow but she couldn't mistake the expression on his face. She smiled at him and he took her hand and pulled her towards him. They danced slowly, close together, out of sync with the rest of the abandoned dancing of the rest of the crowd, then he took her hand a walked up the processional path with her.

The torches put their faces in shadow and in firelight until they came to the Winterfell Stone. They looked at each other and, as one, they reached out and touched the Stone. Warmth shot through Annie's hand and arm, like the heat of the sun on a summer's day. Kit was in front of her, in her thoughts and in reality. She looked across at Kit. They were still holding hands with their other hands still in contact with the Stone. Kit's eyes were closed and then he screwed them together tightly before looking across at Annie.

'It's no good. Whenever I touch this Stone, I can't get anything other than a picture of you in my mind. You won't leave my thoughts. What have you done to me Annie Millford?'

'You are what I see when I touch the Stone, even if I don't want to see you, you are there. Whatever I've done to you, you've done to me' she whispered.

'You know the legend of the Winterfell Stone don't you?' Kit sighed, coming close to Annie. So close.

'I do.' Annie replied, gazing into his eyes.

'We can't escape fate then, can we?' and he swept her towards him and kissed her the way he'd been wanting to forever.

The Stone stood sentinel over them the whole village, as they all danced the dance of times gone by and fulfilled the destiny of ages past.

Lithven Castle
N.W. Highlands
Scotland

*

Darling Christopher,

What wonderful news! I am so glad you are coming up to see us and bringing your lovely Annie with you. It is so exciting that you may be coming up for New Year too – and if I can persuade your grandfather to leave his perch, we would love to come and spend Christmas with you! Thank you! I can't believe it! Although I had high hopes for Annie right from the beginning.

Your grandfather is hanging over my shoulder again (I don't know why he doesn't write his own letter instead of dictating to me!) and says well done on the paper you wrote on the Winterfell Stone Circle. Apparently he says you have made an important discovery and he's very proud of you. As am I of course.

We will see you both in a fortnight's time and please give our love to Annie. Lots of it. I just know I'm going to love her. Your grandfather is grunting that 'she sounds like she'll fit'. High praise indeed! I wish I knew how to do those little smiley-face things on here!

All out love – G and G.

Printed in Great Britain
by Amazon

36099608R00175